Unafraid and Unashamed

Facing the Future of United Methodism

Table of Contents

Dedication

To the United Methodist Church
in which I found Christ
and a community committed
to offering Christ to our world.

Fear

tells us to keep doing
what we have
always done, hoping
the outside world
will go back to the way
it used to be.

Faith

tells a
different story.

Unafraid
and
Unashamed

Facing the Future
of United Methodism

by Robert "Wil" Cantrell

Market Square
BOOKS
Market Square Publishing, LLC
Knoxville, Tennessee

Unafraid and Unashamed

Facing the Future of United Methodism

©2017 Market Square Publishing Company, LLC.
books@marketsquarebooks.com
P.O. Box 23664 Knoxville, Tennessee 37933

ISBN10: 0-9987546-0-9
ISBN13: 978-0-9987546-0-4
Library of Congress: 2017903512

Printed and Bound in the United States of America

Cover Illustration ©2017 Market Square Publishing, LLC
by Kevin Slimp

Foreword

by Bishop David W. Graves

Years ago at a marriage enrichment event for couples, I heard one presenter share that we need to guard our hearts in our relationships with our spouses. There are so many things competing for our time, emotions, and souls that affect the heart. In turn, it could lead us down a road that causes severe pain which moves us away from the ones we so love. Proverbs 3:5 and 6 tell us, "Trust in the Lord with all your heart and lean not on your own understanding; in all your ways submit to him, and he will make your paths straight." (NIV)

The writer of Proverbs goes on to state in verse 7, "Do not be wise in your own eyes." (NIV)

My take on this Proverbs text is that God is saying to each of us, "Guard your heart!"

This theme, "Guard your heart," is one I used with the

Holston Conference delegation as we journeyed together toward the 2016 United Methodist General Conference. It was filled with many pathways. Tensions were building around human sexuality petitions that would be discussed on the floor of the conference.

Several groups were petitioning the General Conference to eliminate the language that appears so harmful to LGBTQ individuals, while others were very much opposed to any change around the language presently contained in *The Book of Discipline.* These kinds of discussions are intense and overwhelming. Emotions get involved which can lead one's spirit to become wounded. Moreover, we can be led down a path toward an undesired destination. Therefore, guard your heart!

Rev. Wil Cantrell and I had been delegates to the 2012 General Conference. It was a real adventure, and I came away with my heart wounded and my soul hurting, primarily because I witnessed so much anger, hurt, and pain in so many others. In 2016, as the first elected clergy delegate, I would be leading our Holston delegation. We had several first-time delegates in our delegation, which ranged in age and theological perspective.

Our Conference had elected a very diverse and Godly group of people. One of my main concerns was that we not only come together for General Conference, but that we return to our homes and congregations stronger for it. Each day, as we were dismissing from our time of prayer to attend committee or plenary sessions, I would remind our group, "Guard your heart!"

Therefore, I would call upon all United Methodists

during this season of waiting for the upcoming 2019 special session of General Conference to guard your hearts. We can get so involved in our own agendas that we move away from having conversations with people who are not like us.

Furthermore, the fear of opening ourselves to others can cause anxiousness that, in turn, can lead to anger and bitterness. We see others as our enemies, aligning against us. In these days, we need to guard our hearts, to focus more on what we have in common, rather than focusing on our differences. We need to keep remain centered on God's sanctifying grace.

Wll Cantrell gives us a practical tool in this book to nurture our faith and guard our hearts as we seek to view our Methodist heritage and live into the future. We have been a people of faith over the past two centuries who have weathered many points of change. This book can serve as a guide to respect viewpoints that differ from our own. By guarding our hearts, we are drawn to focus on our commitment to the local church while weathering our denominational differences.

By guarding our hearts, we can accomplish much for God's kingdom in these days of uncertainty. I highly recommend this book as a must read for all United Methodists.

Bishop David W. Graves
Alabama-West Florida Conference

Introduction
Option: Fear or Faith

A young man with a small problem

My first snap at quarterback in a varsity game did not go as I dreamed. During the first half of a tough game against a good opponent, our starting quarterback got up from a hard tackle with one finger pointing in the wrong direction. As our team trainers worked quickly to straighten his extremity, I ran on the field to take my first snap.

We needed four yards on the next play or we would be forced to punt the ball back to the opposing team from deep within our own territory. While trying to convince the other ten guys in the huddle that I wasn't scared, I looked to the sideline to get the play call. Our coach began the elaborate ritual of sending in the play with secret signals requiring him to be something of a contortionist.

1

After decoding the signals, I did a double-take. I could not believe the play which had been called. I was convinced I had misread the signs.

I looked with bewilderment at the coach and signaled for him to send in the play again. Once more he went through his strange dance sequence, only this time he did it a lot with more emotion, adding a few colorful words.

I watched the signals carefully and I realized my fears were true. I had read the first set of signals correctly. The coach wanted us to run the option.

The option relies on having a quick, athletic quarterback. The play gives the quarterback three options. He can:

1. *immediately hand the ball to the fullback running up the middle of the field;*
2. *keep the ball and run it himself; or*
3. *pitch the ball to the tailback who is running toward the sideline.*

If the defense lines up with a strong presence in the center of the field, preventing the quarterback from giving the ball to the fullback, things begin to get interesting. In an instant the quarterback has to run parallel to the line of scrimmage directly toward one of the biggest, baddest, most dangerous players on the field, the defensive end, and that isn't the worst part.

The defensive end is intentionally left alone on the play. This allows the blockers to focus all of their energies on the other defensive players. It is the quarterback's job to disarm the defensive end using the element of surprise.

He has the option to try to get past the defensive end himself or to pitch the ball to the tailback sprinting alongside him. Since the defensive end has to guard both the quarterback and the tailback, a quarterback with speed can often fake a pitch to the running back and get by the defensive end himself.

On the other hand, if the defensive end comes full speed at the quarterback, the quarterback can pitch the ball to the tailback, who then easily runs past the other defenders.

In theory, the option is one of the simplest and most effective plays in football for a team with a quick athletic quarterback. Unfortunately, I was neither quick nor athletic enough.

In practice my coach often told me, "Wil, we call this play the option. But when you run it, don't think of it as the option. Think of it as the pitch. You're going to pitch the ball. Your job is to get the ball to someone who can actually run fast."

Running a play like the option, especially without a fast quarterback, opens the door for disaster. If my timing was off just slightly, it was possible my wayward pitch would be recovered by the other team or worse yet, the other team would pick the ball up off the ground and run it the other way for a touchdown.

I had hoped my first play might be a short pass for an easy completion or a quick pitch to a running back. I never imagined it would be the option.

Once reality set in, I began to evaluate my own options. I could call time out. However, this decision would draw the ire of my coach and might jeopardize my chances of ever playing quarterback again.

I could call an audible and switch to a different play. This, too, would most likely anger my coach. After all, it was his job, not mine, to pick the plays. I had only one choice: Run the option.

As I brought the team to the line of scrimmage, I hoped the defense would leave the middle of the field uncovered allowing me to hand the ball to the fullback. I had no such luck. The middle of the field was covered tight.

I took stock of my assets. I realized for this one short moment in life, I possessed something I had always wanted, deceptive speed. The defense had no way of knowing how slow I was or that I had no intention of keeping the ball.

I took a deep breath, snapped the ball and ran directly at the unblocked defensive end. To my horror, he initially chose to employ a technique called slow playing. Rather than running immediately at me, which would have allowed me to pitch the ball to the running back, he waited for me to come to him. If I pitched the ball too early he could still adjust his course in time to tackle the tailback. Every second I held on to the ball increased the chances of other defenders arriving in time to stop the play.

I kept running at him. Finally, he came toward me. I pitched the ball just before being driven to the ground. On my way down, I saw the tailback catch the ball and begin running up field.

I wish I could tell you we scored a touchdown on that play. We didn't. We needed four yards for a first down. We got two. We punted on the next play.

Possibly more important, we averted disaster. We kept ourselves in the game and my play gave the coaches confidence to trust me in more important situations later in the season.

The United Methodist Church has been slowly addressing lesbian, gay, bisexual, transgender, and queer/questioning (LGBTQ) issues for more than 40 years. During that time, our demographics, official policies, and cultural perspectives regarding these issues have changed dramatically.

Many of us have shifted our own views significantly, yet our denomination has never been able to arrive at an agreeable consensus in terms of how the church should relate to our LGBTQ brothers and sisters.

While finding a solution that gathers universal support is unlikely, we must be sure we do not allow this conflict to splinter our denomination to such a degree that it has disastrous consequences for our other ministries.

The United Methodist impasse

At the 2016 General Conference in Portland, Oregon, the conflict over LGBTQ inclusion reached its boiling point after simmering for more than four decades. Prior to 2016, most United Methodist leaders wondered how we would resolve our differences regarding the inclusion of LGBTQ persons in our fellowship. Now, many of our lead-

5

ers wonder if our differences can be resolved.

Due to the belief our conflict over full inclusion of LGBTQ persons had reached such an intensity, resulting in not being able to deal with the issue in a fruitful manner, the General Conference appointed the Council of Bishops to set up a special commission. This group was comprised of leaders with diverse perspectives, from diverse parts of the world. Their mission was to work together to find a way forward.

This commission, made up of 32 UMC leaders from around the world, began its work in the autumn of 2016. As of this writing, no formal proposals have come from the commission. The Council of Bishops, however, has indicated its intent to call a special General Conference session in early 2019 to deal directly with the recommendations of the commission.

As United Methodists, we find ourselves in a situation similar to, but infinitely more serious than, the situation I found myself in many years ago. We have several options before us. Some lead to disaster. Others to fruitfulness.

For some of us, this may not be that for which we bargained. We hoped our church wouldn't move this direction on our watch.

We wanted to reach the world for Christ. We wanted to help our church tackle global problems like hunger, health, education, and women's rights. We wanted to lead spiritual awakenings in secular societies and revivals in religious cultures.

What we didn't want was to spend our time wrestling with the struggle of whether the United Methodist

Church should remain united.

For others of us, the struggle for social justice, combined with our perspective on biblical interpretation and authority, is exactly how we want to spend our lives.

We hoped for the full support of our church. We hoped our struggle would instill values into a broken and hurting world, rather than forcing us to fight to instill them into a divided and hurting church.

Often life teaches us hard lessons. Sometimes we can pick our battles. Other times, our battles pick us, and our only option is to determine the methods we will use.

The battle for the soul of United Methodism will not be fought against other United Methodists of differing perspectives. It won't be fought against caucus groups, the standing rules of General Conference or the Judicial Council. It will not be determined by interpretations of The Book of Discipline, or the Bishops' implementation of discipline.

The battle for the soul of United Methodism will be fought against powers and principalities. It will be a struggle between the power of fear and the power of faith.

The Bible is full of stories of people who had to choose between fear and faith. From Abraham's repeated attempts to pass his wife off as his sister, to the decision of the disciples to abandon Jesus after his arrest, we see clearly the tragic consequences of living out of fear. Yet, Abraham and the disciples also show us the miraculous power resulting from living out of faith.

The same Abraham who tried to pass his wife off as his sister believed God could give him descendants who would bless all the nations of the world. The same disciples who deserted Jesus later chose to risk their lives to bring the Gospel to a world in need of grace only Christ could supply.

Long after Abraham, and well before Jesus' disciples came on the scene, there was a powerful young man wrestling with the power of fear and the power of faith. His battle would forever alter the political landscape of the ancient world.

A young man with a big problem

Rehoboam became king of Israel after his father Solomon passed away sometime in the 920s BCE. His story is told in 1 Kings 11:43-14:31 and 2 Chronicles 9:31-12:16.

Around the time of Rehoboam's ascension to the throne, the military prowess and political power of Israel reached its peak just as the old divisions between the northern and southern tribes bubbled to the surface.

The divisions between the tribes stretched as far back as the beginning of David's reign. In 2 Samuel 2-5 the story is told of how David, Rehoboam's grandfather, united the southern kingdom of Judah and the northern kingdom of Israel.

After King Saul's death, the southern tribes quickly anointed David as the new King of Judah. The northern tribes, however, chose to install Saul's son, Ishbaal, as king.

Seven years of conflict between the southern tribes, led by King David, and the northern tribes, under the command of King Ishbaal, ensued. When Ishbaal died, the leaders of the northern tribes met with King David at Hebron to negotiate an arrangement, restoring unity to the kingdom by making David king of all Israel.

Though the Bible provides only scant details, we can imagine the northern kingdom had to give up certain powers to David they would have preferred to keep. By the same token, David probably had to make concessions to the northern tribes regarding specific issues crucial to them.

During the reigns of King David and his son King Solomon, the rising political and economic fortunes of Israel kept tensions at bay. As economic growth slowed during the end of Solomon's reign, the divisions between north and south now reemerged more strongly than ever.

Near the end of Solomon's reign, several rivals sought to usurp his power. The most dangerous threat came from Jeroboam. While serving Solomon with distinction, Jeroboam came to believe a prophecy which revealed God would take control of the ten northern tribes from Solomon, making Jeroboam king of the north. Solomon soon learned of Jeroboam's ambitions and forced him to seek exile in Egypt.

Consider the pressures a young Rehoboam would have felt as he ascended to the throne of his father. Suddenly he was responsible for overseeing the continued growth of the kingdom with an unprecedented infrastructure. At the same time, rivals were trying to overthrow his regime.

If Rehoboam did not lead strongly, his opponents

would interpret his actions as weakness and become emboldened to attack him. Without a show of strength, he might fail to inspire the tribes to continue working on the nation's massive infrastructure. If he led too strongly, he risked straining the fragile alliance between the northern and southern tribes past the breaking point.

As Rehoboam looked out over all of Israel who had gathered at Shechem to anoint him king, I imagine Rehoboam felt one overwhelming emotion: Fear.

Rehoboam quickly discovered the tribes had no intention of granting him the monarchy until they were successful in renegotiating the balance between the centralized power of the monarchy and the local power of the tribes.

The tribes demanded Rehoboam lower the high taxes and lessen the amount of conscripted servitude demanded by Solomon. No doubt, Rehoboam was hoping for a more benign coronation. Instead, his power was being tested before he even began his reign. He was facing his worst fear.

Initially, Rehoboam exhibited great wisdom in his response to such a troubling political quandary. He asked for time to consider the options. He consulted with his father's advisers, the older and wiser leaders of the kingdom. These men understood the needs of the kingdom while also sympathizing with the tribes.

They were seasoned advisors who knew the resources needed to maintain the existing infrastructure. They realized maintaining what they had was much easier than building it from scratch.

Moreover, they recognized concessions to the tribes could engender great loyalty to Rehoboam. Not surprisingly, they advised their king to grant the request of the tribes to lessen their burdens.

Next, Rehoboam talked to a group of young advisers who had grown up with him in the halls of power. Eager to create their own legacy, these young men pushed for Rehoboam to deal harshly with the tribes.

If Israel were to reach new levels of power, it would need new levels of commitment from the tribes. In their minds, any compromise with the tribes would show weakness.

Ultimately, Rehoboam's fear of coming across as weak led him to side with his younger friends rather than his father's more experienced advisors. After three days of deliberations, Rehoboam stood before Israel to reveal his policies would be harsher than his father's.

Taxes would be higher. Conscripted labor would be greater. Penalties for failing to support the kingdom would be stiffer. You can imagine how that went over.

The northern tribes of Israel immediately anointed Jeroboam as their king and split from the southern tribes of Judah. The southern tribes eventually anointed Rehoboam king. While Judah maintained control over Jerusalem, his kingdom now consisted of only two tribes, Judah and Benjamin.

In an effort to promote allegiance within the northern kingdom, King Jeroboam instructed the people to stop offering sacrifices at the temple in Jerusalem.

Instead, he fashioned idols for the people to worship in their own lands.

This willingness to forsake their faith in the one true God in favor of more politically expedient idols led to idolatry and polytheism. Perhaps it was the watered down religion of the northern kingdom which ultimately led the citizens of the northern kingdom to cease for all time to be identifiable as Israelites. In the years following the invasion of the Assyrians in 740 BCE, the northern tribes would adopt so many of the religious and cultural practices of the Assyrians they would cease to be Israelites altogether.

Judah, though greatly weakened politically by the secession of the northern tribes, maintained worship of the one true God with varying degrees of faithfulness. Their common belief in the one true God enabled them to rebuild their nation after the Babylonian exile.

This created a culture in which vibrant forms of Judaism could flourish even as the nation of Judah came under the control of the surrounding empires. It was into such a politically weak, but religiously strong, Judah that Jesus was born centuries later.

Imagine how history would be different if Rehoboam had responded out of faith rather than fear. Next consider what is at stake in our response to the current crisis in the United Methodist Church. Will we respond out of fear or out of faith?

Like the kingdoms of old, will we feel the need to differentiate ourselves from our brothers and sisters of differing viewpoints to such an extent we sacrifice the power of our shared ministry?

Will local churches be split apart due to differing beliefs regarding the inclusion of LGBTQ persons? Will we bear such resentment toward those within United Methodism who disagree with us that our expressions of worship will become little more than liturgies for the like-minded?

Will we fight out our differences in secular courts rather than finding a way to live out an expression of church that is in line with our collective conscience? Will we realize John's Wesley's greatest fear, that we become "dead sects, having the form of religion, without the power?"

Or will we find a way to respond in faith that allows us to live out John Wesley's vision for why God raised up the people called Methodist in the first place, "To reform the nation, particularly the church, and to spread scriptural holiness?"

Jesus, John Wesley, and scriptural holiness

Regardless of whether we find a way to continue to reside within the same denominational polity, we will continue to have the opportunity to respond to the needs and controversies of our contemporary world in a way that spreads scriptural holiness.

Scriptural holiness calls us to the highest standard. It is a higher standard than orthodoxy. It calls us to a greater goal than even social justice, which leads to life giving social policies. While the importance of beliefs and social justice cannot be overstated, scriptural holiness is even more central within the life of Christ than beliefs or policies.

Consider what we know of Jesus from the Gospel accounts. Jesus spent much of his life teaching the truth about God. If Jesus' primary goal was providing a pure understanding of systematic theology, however, he would have been better served by teaching his followers to memorize a detailed outline of God's nature. Instead, he told parables and ate with sinners.

Jesus took significant amounts of time lifting up the downcast and outcast. There's no question Jesus' life has many political implications for the church and society at large. But if Jesus' primary goal had been a perfectly just social order, why not create a tightly coordinated political party to challenge Rome for political control of the Mediterranean world?

Jesus was quite controversial in his day because he did not make his ministry simply about correct theology. The Pharisees did that.

Jesus caught a lot of criticism for failing to form his followers into a political movement. Many people thought the messiah was supposed to do just that.

Instead, Jesus lifted up two values above theology and correct social policies: Loving God and loving our neighbor. It was these overarching values John Wesley referred to as "scriptural holiness".

The reason scriptural holiness resonates so strongly with us is because it bears so much resemblance to the example of Christ. The vision of scriptural holiness refers to the quality of our relationships.

Scriptural holiness calls to us to a standard so high it exposes our sinfulness and selfish nature. It is easier to believe correctly about God than to be in right relationship with God. It is much simpler to advocate for ethical social policies than to love our neighbors as we love ourselves.

Jesus' focus on scriptural holiness offends many of our well-cultivated religious sensibilities. We love that he ate with tax collectors, prostitutes, and sinners. We wish he had not included slave owners, bigots, and assassins in his fellowship.

We are glad Jesus taught the truth about God, but we struggle with how to understand the story of the Good Samaritan, in which a person with unorthodox religious beliefs is celebrated as a beacon of faithfulness.

I can't tell you with certainty how we will resolve the impasse over the full inclusion of LGBTQ persons in our fellowship. I can't even guarantee such solutions can be found.

Like everyone, I have my opinions. I am sure you have yours, too. I pray, as a result of thousands of conversations over the next two to three years, solutions will come to light.

Could it be God is using this current crisis to call us all back to the high vision of scriptural holiness?

I pray we find the courage to look fully at our differences through the lens of our shared beliefs, our beloved means of grace, and our desire to love others as God has first loved us.

This book lays out my conviction in which common beliefs, our Wesleyan means of grace, and our God-given desire to love our neighbors can guide us into a bright future.

If we find within ourselves the courage to set aside our fears and embark on this journey, then perhaps the people called United Methodists will discover a miraculous capacity to share hope, healing, and joy with a hurting and divided world.

As John Wesley would say, we will find ourselves spreading "scriptural holiness over the land."

Chapter One

Removing the
Rose Colored Glasses

*Our emotional attachment to the status quo
often causes us to look at our church
through rose colored glasses.*

To say I am emotionally attached to United Methodism is a little like saying Jamaican sprinter Usain Bolt is fast.

My paternal grandfather ("Pop") grew up in a Methodist Episcopal Church, South congregation in the small town of Alexandria, Tennessee. Shortly after he left home for college, his father passed away and he was forced to return home to take care of his mother. During the great depression, he took a job with the Civilian Conservation Corp to assist with his mother's needs back home.

He didn't get to go to college, but it seemed like everyone who knew him thought he would have ended up being a lawyer or a preacher, given the opportunity.

As it turned out, he married my grandmother and began working in the newly constructed nuclear plants of Oak Ridge, Tennessee. They soon began attending a new

17

Methodist church, meeting in a movie theater. During his career, he carefully hoarded vacation days for three of his paramount priorities: trips with family, World Series games, and annual conference in Lake Junaluska, North Carolina. Some years he was a delegate. Other times he went on his own. Either way, he always attended the Holston Annual Conference and followed the proceedings closely.

Whenever I visited my grandparents, the dinner table conversations were filled with Pop's stories about the churches, pastors, and bishops he knew. His dramatic tone turned each story into a hysterical sequence of events, a shameful act of ignorance, or a profound example of faithful Christian living. When I spent evenings at his home, I would stare at a bookshelf full of all the Holston Annual Conference journals. He had them all, in order by year, going all the way back to the 1950s.

My father heard a call to ministry during his college years and eventually became an ordained elder - our official term for clergyperson - in the Holston Conference. I grew up moving from parsonage to parsonage in my early years.

Like my father, I attended college planning to be an engineer, but plans changed and I emerged from college with a call to ordained ministry. At seminary, I struggled to relate to classmates who enrolled without a clear sense of calling. I knew exactly why I was going to seminary several years before I arrived, to be a United Methodist Minister. Their confusion confused me.

When people ask me about my hometown, I take a

deep breath and tell them: "My home town begins in the Appalachian coalfields of Southwest Virginia where there is a river with three forks. The middle and the south fork merge just a few miles outside of Abingdon, Virginia, then flow toward Kingsport, Tennessee where they combine with the North Fork to form the Holston River. Flowing south toward Knoxville, the Holston River and French Broad River converge to create the Tennessee River. The Tennessee River runs south through Chattanooga and shortly thereafter leaves God's country. That river marks my home. From Southwest Virginia through Chattanooga is where I call home."

As you might have guessed, the area I have just described corresponds to the geographic boundaries of the Holston Conference of the United Methodist Church.

Needless to say, I am very fond of our current United Methodist structure. I intellectually understand the world-wide Church is bigger than United Methodism, but United Methodism has always been my church world. I know there are many diverse brands of churches in East Tennessee and Southwest Virginia, but the Holston Conference has always been my church home. As a result, any conversation which hints at a reconfiguring of our structure causes my stomach to churn.

You might have a strong emotional connection to our configuration as well. Perhaps you have been at the same church for decades and the thought of conflict within the congregation you love so dearly pains you deeply. Maybe you have worked in ministry with other churches in your district and you cannot imagine not being closely aligned in ministry with nearby United Methodist churches. It is possible that you have worked through Volunteers in Mission with United Methodist churches in far-away lands. The last thing you want to do is put our global connections in peril.

There is a chance you are like me. Maybe you have moved around quite a bit. In each new place you have needed a church home and you always found a United Methodist church that was just the right place for you.

In each new setting, you found comfort in seeing the cross and flame on the sign and knowing inside you would most likely find strong theology and thoughtful compassionate ethics taught from the pulpit, warm fellowship, Sunday School classes that teach and practice loving our neighbors, and mission opportunities to help meet the greatest needs of the community.

It's possible you have been in theologically conservative United Methodist churches and in liberal United Methodist churches. If you are like me, you have felt the unmistakable love of Christ in each.

You may have a different story. Maybe you have lived outside the church for many years. Perhaps you realized your life was missing something foundational and turned to a United Methodist church. In that congregation, you found faith, forgiveness, saving grace, acceptance, meaning, and purpose for the first time. For you, church is truly a sanctuary from a world in which people often mistreat each other and where the dominant cultural attitudes lead to narcissistic self-centered living.

When the preacher talks about living as citizens of the

Kingdom of Heaven while sojourning here on earth, you get it. For you this is what church is all about, so when you hear there are conflicts in your denomination threatening its unity, you worry. The idea of Christians speaking ill of one another makes you feel like throwing your hands in the air and crying.

Conflict, rivalry, and mistrust are the ways of the world. They are not supposed to be the ways of the church.

Our emotional attachment to the status quo or revulsion with church conflict often causes us to look at our church through rose colored glasses. The problem with rose colored glass, which country singer John Conlee reminded the world of in his classic song of the same title, is that rose colored glasses tend to show us what we want to see, rather than what is really there.

Most everyone has a tendency to look at things they love through rose colored glasses. When we look at our denomination or local church, it's easy to see only what we want to see. Doing anything else reveals our bumps and bruises, not just its beauty.

This habit of looking through rose colored glasses is common in churches of every size and type. I have heard churches describe themselves as "strong and growing" while shedding members and money for years. I have visited churches who pride themselves in their children's ministry, but don't have a single baby in the nursery.

Even when churches recognize their challenges, it is tempting to jump immediately to quick solutions which gloss over the real issues, but rarely solve anything.

Many times, when confronted with a problem, the initial response is to put more resources towards an existing ministry which often had been quite successful ten or twenty years earlier.

There's a reason programs and ministries come and go. While some decline due to poor oversight, most eventually fade when the needs of persons and families change. Perhaps the only way to make lasting positive change is to seek to understand how the cultural context of the church's community has changed. With that understanding we have a better chance of finding or creating ministries to fit the new context.

It is frightening to take a wide-eyed look at reality when that reality threatens the cherished institutions and traditions that have shaped our character and our souls. Fear tells us to look away.

Fear tells us to keep doing what we have always done and hope the outside world will go back to the way it used to be.

Faith tells a different story.

Faith tells us Jesus is the solid rock when we reach rock bottom. Faith tells us that God's best work occurs in a graveyard.

Faith tells us it is only when we look at reality with wide eyes that we see the depth of our problems. Faith tells us our challenges pale in comparison to the depth of the love and power of our God.

In the following chapters, I invite you to look with me at the depth of division within United Methodism. Much of our division is centered around LGBTQ inclusion and our tendency to forget God is ready and able to lead us to a faithful future.

Unlikely converts

The more I read the Bible, the more I learn to look for hope and inspiration in unlikely places. Of all places, I find a lot of hope in the story surrounding the people of Nineveh.

Jonah's story is short, action-packed, and children love it. Let's face it. What's not to love about the story of man who is called by God to preach to people he hates, runs from God, gets on a boat, encounters a storm on the open seas and gets thrown overboard?

How could anyone not love a story which ends with Jonah being swallowed by a big fish, living in its stomach for three days, praying to God for deliverance, and is subsequently regurgitated onto dry land?

No wonder he captures our attention when he preaches to the people he hates and leads them to repentance, becoming so enraged by God's mercy toward them he becomes depressed and contemplates taking his own life. Ultimately he hears God's own voice describe God's love for people who seemingly do not deserve it.

The character of Jonah is so fascinating, we immediately see this story from his point of view. I would like to challenge you to take out your Bibles and read the book of Jonah again. It won't take long. Jonah takes up only two pages in most Bibles. This time when you read Jonah, don't think of it as the story of Jonah. Think of it as the story of Nineveh. Imagine it from the perspective of a resident of Nineveh.

In Jonah 1:2 God tells Jonah, "Go to the great city of Nineveh and preach against it, because its wickedness has come up before me." (NIV)

There is good reason for God to call Nineveh great. Nineveh had been an influential city in the Assyrian empire since 2600BCE. In Jonah's days in the 8th Century BCE, Nineveh was on its way to becoming the largest city in the known world.

We learn in Jonah 4:11 Nineveh had more than 120,000 people in it. Historical investigation estimates this number to be fairly accurate which makes Nineveh much larger than Babylon or any other city in the region at the time. This is where Jonah goes to preach.

"Nineveh is an exceedingly large city, a three days' walk across." (Jonah 3:3, NIV)

Jonah probably could have walked straight through Nineveh in one day, but if he wanted to stop and preach in each borough, it very likely would have taken three days to do so.

We think of Nineveh as a backward evil place as a result of Jonah's disdain for it. No city becomes the largest city in the world, however, without a community of industrious leaders dedicated to planning, protecting, enhancing, and maintaining the city's culture and infrastructure. Most likely, some of the greatest artists, thinkers, and craftsmen in the ancient world resided in Nineveh during this time.

What could be so wrong with the people of Nineveh to cause Jonah to hate them and God to feel an urgent need to call them to repentance, describing them as "people who cannot tell their right hand from their left" (Jonah 4:11, NIV)?

Nineveh's greatest crime may have been its position as the religious base for worship of Mesopotamian goddess Ishtar. Or it could be that Nineveh was hated because of the power of the Assyrian empire and the atrocities committed by its conquering soldiers. Regardless, the situation in Nineveh had gotten bad enough God decided the Ninevites must repent or their city would be no more.

From the perspective of the citizens of Nineveh, I imagine things looked pretty nice prior to Jonah's unannounced preaching tour. They were the largest city in the world with the nicest architecture. The wealth and power of the Assyrian empire was growing and their wealth increased exponentially as the spoils of war flowed into the city gates.

It is difficult to imagine the Ninevites felt they had anything to learn from an unknown prophet from Israel, their weak neighbor to the South.

Yet, when the people of Nineveh heard Jonah preaching repentance, they did the strangest thing. They repented. From the king to the lowliest servant, they all repented and prayed for God to have mercy on them.

I have no idea why the Ninevites responded with repentance rather than revulsion to Jonah's message. But I find a lot of hope in their response. Here they were, the residents of the most powerful city on earth, hearing a foreign message. They were warned. If they kept living like they had been, their lifestyles would lead to destruction. Amazingly, they set aside their pride and prayerfully began changing their lives.

Going further, if you read the book of Nahum you will learn Nineveh eventually went back to its old ways and ultimately faced destruction a little more than a hundred years later. Still, for more than a century after Jonah, Nineveh continued as a center of power, commerce, and art due to their sincere repentance.

If the people of Nineveh, who did not know their right hand from their left, can take an unflinching look at their lives and ask God how they need to be different, can we as United Methodist do less?

For many of us, General Conference 2016 was our Jonah moment. In Portland, we realized we could not keep on going down the same path and expect everything to be okay.

A brief history of a long struggle

The debate surrounding LGBTQ inclusion formally began in the United Methodist Church in 1972. After the Methodist Church and the Evangelical United Brethren merged to form the United Methodist Church in 1968, a committee was assigned to bring back suggested changes to The Social Principles contained in The Book of Discipline to the next General Conference to be held in Atlanta, Georgia.

Considering the social upheaval in the United States during the 1960s and the reality of a newly merged, increasingly diverse denomination, 1972 was a logical time for the United Methodist Church to ensure The

Social Principles expressed the most current sentiments within United Methodism. One of the changes presented to the General Conference in 1972 stated:

> "Homosexuals, no less than heterosexuals, are persons of sacred worth, who need the ministry and guidance of the church in their struggles for human fulfillment, as well as the spiritual and emotional care of a fellowship which enables reconciling relationships with God, with others and with self. Further, we insist that all persons are entitled to have their human and civil rights ensured."

After substantial debate, the phrase "We do not condone the practice of homosexuality and consider it incompatible with Christian teaching" was added to this section of The Social Principles. A statement on homosexual unions was also adopted which said, "We do not recommend marriage between two persons of the same sex."

At this beginning of the United Methodist debate on homosexuality, two themes emerge that have been a part of the official United Methodist position on homosexuality ever since. First, the belief gay and lesbian people are persons of sacred worth who need their human and civil rights protected. Second, homosexuality was viewed as "incompatible with Christian teaching".

Interestingly, though in today's verbiage we often group issues concerning LGBTQ persons together, United Methodist polity has not followed this format. You may have noticed the 1972 General Conference did not officially address transsexuality. United Methodist polity clearly lays out several positions relating to homosexuality, however issues concerning transsexuality are left up to the annual conferences in regards to ordination and to local churches and their pastors in regards to marriage.

If you would like a more detailed account of the legislative debates of each General Conference since 1972 surrounding homosexuality, I would instruct you to view the excellent slide show put together by Kathy Gilbert of the United Methodist News Service which can be found on umc.org[1]. For the purposes of this book, I would like to focus on some of the major momentum shifts within the General Conference debates.

During the **1980 General Conference in Indianapolis**, language opposing same sex unions was removed from The Discipline and an effort to ban "self-avowed practicing homosexuals" from being ordained was defeated. However, at the **1984 Baltimore General Conference,** "self-avowed practicing homosexuals" were banned from being ordained or appointed to serve in any clergy role within the UMC.

While those with a progressive mindset likely hoped the votes at the 1980 General Conference were a sign greater degrees of inclusion would be adopted in the years to come, the 1984 General Conference clearly demonstrated the denomination was moving in a more conservative direction.

Another resounding defeat for progressive views occurred in the **1992 Louisville General Conference**. Following statements which affirmed God's grace is available to all and directing the United Methodist Church to be in ministry with all persons, a study

---

1 umc.org/news-and-media/gc2016-tackling-44-year-stance-on-homosexuality

commission was set up to bring recommendations to the 1992 General Conference pertaining to how to be in ministry with homosexual persons.

Once again, progressives hoped the study commission would lead the denomination to move towards full inclusion of homosexual persons. However, in Louisville, delegates voted 710-238 (75%-25%) to retain the statement describing homosexuality as incompatible with Christian teaching.

While some might have seen the Louisville vote as definitive, again there was a swing back toward the progressive direction at the **1996 Denver General Conference**. Another attempt was made to repeal the language of incompatibility, but once again it was defeated.

This time, though, the vote was 577-378. Moving from a 75-25 vote to a 60-40 vote in just four years seemed to many like a harbinger of more progressive policies in the future.

The **2000 General Conference in Cleveland** and the **2004 General Conference in Pittsburgh** produced some of the most painful moments in our denominational struggle. In Cleveland, progressive protests occurred which resulted in the arrests of more than 200 people including two United Methodist Bishops.

In Pittsburgh, as part of the protests, a communion chalice was broken. The image of the broken chalice became an emotional touchstone within United Methodism. To some, it poignantly symbolized the brokenness of a denomination that deems each person to be of sacred worth, yet denies some people the sacred chance to share their gifts fully in ministry.

To others, it is seen as a sacrilegious image, producing suspicion of groups within the progressive movement. They feel these groups have made LGBTQ inclusion a greater priority than the church's mission of making disciples of Jesus Christ.

Somehow, even during these painful conferences, United Methodists of varying perspectives worked together to produce two of the more important statements to come out of the decades long debate.

In Cleveland, the sentence, "We implore families and churches not to reject or condemn their lesbian and gay members and friends," was added to The Social Principles during an era when increasing openness among LGBTQ persons was leading to increasing persecution within the United States.

Four years later in Pittsburgh in the aftermath of the arrests and the broken chalice, there was talk of a split in the denomination.

In response, delegates passed a Unity Resolution with an overwhelming vote of 869-41. It read:

> "As United Methodists, we remain in covenant with one
> another, even in the midst of our disagreement, and affirm
> our commitment to work together for the common mission of
> making disciples throughout the world."

During the decades of the 1990s and 2000s, a telling trend emerged in General Conference debates. General Conference is divided into two weeks. Any legislation that makes it to the floor of the General Conference for debate during the second week must first be brought to the floor by the legislative committee assigned to consider it during the first week.

In these years, progressive legislation related to LGBTQ inclusion often came to the floor with support from its legislative committee. Once it reached the floor, however, it was defeated or replaced with more conservative language while being debated by the full General Conference.

The legislative committee votes caused many within United Methodism to believe more LGBTQ inclusion was inevitable, which produced optimism among progressive voices and caused more conservative United Methodists to wonder how long they could remain in the denomination.

This trend continued until the **2012 General Conference in Tampa, Florida.** At the Tampa conference, legislation came to the floor through a minority report of the legislative committee to change the language stating that homosexuality is incompatible with Christianity and replace it with a statement recognizing the differences of opinion within United Methodism regarding LGBTQ inclusion.

As part of the debate, Rev. Adam Hamilton and Rev. Mike Slaughter, two widely respected pastors in the denomination, with deep connections to progressive, moderate, and conservative constituencies, spoke in favor of language that recognized the genuine disagreement over LGBTQ inclusion. For many people, this seemed like the watershed moment when the historic opposition to homosexuality in The Discipline would be changed.

Once more, no such change occurred. Following the

narrow defeat (47% for and 51% against) of the legislation put forward by Rev. Hamilton and Rev. Slaughter, other similar legislative proposals were soundly defeated. After these votes, protests immediately shut down the work of the General Conference and all remaining legislation relating to human sexuality was tabled indefinitely in an effort to restore order to the General Conference.

After 2012, some saw United Methodism beginning to move back toward a more conservative direction. Others, buoyed by the narrow defeat of the Hamilton/Slaughter proposal and historic civil right gains for the LGBTQ community in the United States, believed the 2016 General Conference would move the UMC in a more progressive direction. These progressive hopes were further stoked in 2015 by recommendations coming from the Connectional Table, the highest ranking body charged with guiding the denomination between General Conferences. The Connectional Table called for allowing pastors and churches to decide whether to perform same-sex weddings and to allow annual conferences to decide the standards for ordination in regards to human sexuality.

By the time the **2016 General Conference** began in Portland, Oregon, concern for the unity of the United Methodist Church ran high as plans coming from conservative constituencies calling for an "amicable separation" were gaining traction with a much broader audience. During the first week of the conference, a series of procedural votes as well as votes within legislative committees confirmed that a growing majority of delegates held conservative positions on issues of LGBTQ inclusion.

Leaders recognized a floor debate could lead to protests, resulting in a complete shutdown of the General Conference. In addition, facing the possibility of a poorly orchestrated split within United Methodism occurring during the final week of General Conference, delegates took the unprecedented step of asking the Council of Bishops to propose a way forward for the denomination.

The Bishops responded by recommending a special commission be set up to study the issue with the possibility of calling a special session of General Conference to be convened in 2018 or 2019 for the sole purpose of dealing with the conflict surrounding LGBTQ inclusion. The Bishops' plan was narrowly adopted (428 – 405). In the fall of 2016, the special commission was formed and began its work with hopes for a special session of General Conference to be held in February or March of 2019 dealing solely with these issues.

At this point, you might be wondering how so many people of various perspectives, believing more progressive policies within United Methodism were inevitable, could have miscalculated so dramatically. How could the United Methodist Church move in a conservative direction while the broader society moved in a more progressive direction? What happened? What changed?

What changed were the demographics of our denomination. As the culture of the United States has become more inclusive of LGBTQ persons, so has a growing percentage of United Methodists within the United States. However, the United Methodist Church has seen a significant decline in the membership in the United States which is especially pronounced in geographical areas which tend to be most progressive. At the same time, United Methodism has experienced tremendous growth in Africa where social standards for human sexuality are much more conservative.

In 2008, the United Methodist Church welcomed the former Protestant Methodist Church of Côte d'Ivoire and its 700,000 members into the UMC. This merger accelerated the changing demographics of General Conference delegates who are selected from the annual conferences based on the membership of their annual conferences.

In 2016, 58% of delegates came from the United States and 30% came from Africa. As recently as 1995, 88% of all United Methodists resided in the United States. As our demographics have changed so too have our voting trends.

Is the UMC still United Methodist?

In the time since the 2016 General Conference, much has happened. The Western Jurisdiction, elected and consecrated Rev. Karen Oliveto, a married lesbian woman, to the office of Bishop. Many progressive voices hailed Bishop Oliveto's election as an act of "Biblical obedience," even if it meant being disobedient to The Discipline which contains the policies and church laws of the denomination.

Others saw Bishop Oliveto's election as exhibiting blatant disregard for the shared covenant of the United Methodist Church and wondered how to stay in covenant with those who openly and joyfully break the agreement.

Meanwhile conservative groups of United Methodists

formed the Wesleyan Covenant Association. Its found-
ers celebrated the Wesleyan Covenant Association as,
"an alliance to advance vibrant, scriptural Christianity
within Methodism," where evangelical, orthodox United
Methodists could come together to encourage and support
one another in their shared ministry.[2]

On the other hand, substantial numbers of moderate
and progressive United Methodists viewed the Wesleyan
Covenant Association as working to create the infrastructure necessary to separate from the United Methodist
Church and form a new more conservative Methodist
denomination.

The glorious dream of United Methodism is to be a
denomination of diverse voices united by shared beliefs
in basic Christian tenets, Wesleyan views of grace, and
the shared covenant established by Methodist church
polity.

With progressive groups openly violating our methods
for church organization and conservative groups calling
for "amicable separation," United Methodists now must
confront a fateful question:

Is the United Methodist Church,
as it is currently constituted,
still "United" or "Methodist?"

---

2   www.wesleyancovenant.org

Chapter Two

Paying the Cover Charge

"In the essentials unity, in the non-essentials liberty,
in all things charity."

1626, **Paraenesis votiva pro Pace Ecclesiae ad Theologos Augustanae Confessionis**
Rupertus Meldenius, 17th Century German Lutheran Theologian

When I was younger I would occasionally visit music establishments requiring a cover charge. In deciding which bands to hear, I would ask myself three questions: Is this band decent? Is the cover charge too much? Will they finish playing before the sun comes up? If the answer to any of those questions was no, I usually passed. It just was not worth it to me.

Some of my friends were willing to pay much higher cover charges. They really appreciated good music. They could hear lead and bass lines working together. They appreciated the intricacies of a well-rehearsed rhythm section and of a vocalist's smooth passagio. These friends would scour the local paper to see who was playing where each week. In their minds, no cover charge was too much if the right band were in town.

Now I am at a different stage of life in which a night out also involves a hefty babysitting fee. My willingness to pay a cover charge for a late night concert has gone from sporadic to non-existent. My more musically inclined friends, however, assure me such performances still take place and they still pay whatever it costs to hear the music they love.

Offering a helpful voice within the United Methodist dialogue concerning LGBTQ inclusion requires paying a high cover charge. When this price goes unpaid or under-paid, our voices become divisive and harmful. The cover cost includes being able to articulate the viewpoints of those across the theological spectrum in a sincerely chari-table and authentically Christian manner.

A willingness to pay this price creates a platform of trust allowing us to offer our personal views in a way that invites dialogue and learning, rather than furthering the already deep divide. Admittedly, this cover charge is more difficult to pay for those on either far end of the spectrum. Yet, when those on the extremes are willing to articulate the other side of the argument in a sincerely charita-ble manner, it creates an exponentially greater positive impact than when someone with a more moderate posi-tion conveys the same message.

The highest cover charge ever paid

Understanding how a particular situation affects everyone was a skill fulfilled by Jesus. Consider how

Hebrews 4 describes the source of Jesus' authority.

> 14 Therefore, since we have a great high priest who has ascended into heaven, Jesus the Son of God, let us hold firmly to the faith we profess. 15 For we do not have a high priest who is unable to empathize with our weaknesses, but we have one who has been tempted in every way, just as we are—yet he did not sin. 16 Let us then approach God's throne of grace with confidence, so that we may receive mercy and find grace to help us in our time of need." (NIV)

According to the author of Hebrews, Jesus earned the right to be our authority by enduring the same temptations as us, yet living without sin. We can bristle at some of Jesus' teachings. We can struggle with how to apply Jesus' guidance in our busy, complex lives. We can question whether certain sayings of Jesus were meant literally or figuratively.

Still, at the end of the day, Jesus is the only person who knows every temptation we encounter, every struggle we face. He understands every pain we bear, every joy in our heart, and every dream we hold dear.

Oh, by the way, he is not only the only person to ever live a sinless life but he is also the only one to come down from heaven and the only one to come back from the dead. He alone has the authority to teach us the mystery of life, death, and life beyond death.

To help us consider the lengths Christ went to pay his cover charge, I'd like to ask you to join in an exercise I often share with teenagers at our church.

First, think of the nicest place you have ever stayed, with the most comfortable accommodations. Maybe it was an immaculate residence overlooking the crystal clear ocean, or perhaps a five-star hotel with attendants waiting to take care of any possible need. Perhaps it was a swanky get-away retreat where you slept on 2,000 thread count sheets and ate expensive dinners. If you love being out-doors, you might think about sleeping in your hammock on a warm night, listening to the sounds of nature and watching the sun rise over the mountains.

Next, imagine the worst, most uncomfortable place you have ever stayed. Maybe it was a cold, tile floor during a mission trip. What about a dirt floor? Do you know what is like to live in 100-degree heat without air conditioning? Do you know what it is like to be cold to your bones, knowing tomorrow won't be any warmer? Have you spent a night in jail and lived in the hopeless-ness of knowing every move you made required someone else's permission?

Given the choice to live out your days in the nicest place you have ever been or in the most difficult place, what would it take to for you to choose the most uncom-fortable option?

Speaking of Jesus, John 1:3 tells us, "Through him all things were made; without him nothing was made that has been made." (NIV)

Before his birth in Bethlehem, Jesus resided in the heavens. He could look out over all of creation. He could gaze into the glories of the galaxies anytime he liked. He felt no physical pain. He resided in a paradise our wildest imaginations cannot fathom.

Then, he gave it up. He gave it up to live in a small shack with a dirt floor and no indoor plumbing in ancient

Palestine. He chose to be hot in the summer, cold in the winter, and sore year-round from his work as a carpenter.

What's more, John goes on to tell us, "He came to that which was his own, but his own did not receive him." (John 1:11, NIV)

Prior to his birth in Bethlehem, he enjoyed unbroken communion with the Father and the Holy Spirit. On Earth, he would be confused, frustrated, and betrayed by those who knew him best.

Finally, one day on a hill outside Jerusalem, he would feel his fellowship with the Father severed as his tortured body began to succumb to the horror of crucifixion.

Philippians 2:6-8 describes Jesus' choice to sacrifice for us with these famous words:

> 6 Who, being in very nature God, did not consider equality with God something to be used to his own advantage;
> 7 rather, he made himself nothing by taking the very nature of a servant, being made in human likeness.
> 8 And being found in appearance as a man, he humbled himself by becoming obedient to death – even death on a cross! (NIV)

What would could cause the Son of God to make such a choice?

Only love.

Through his sinless life, in which he was tempted in every way, Jesus paid the price to be our Lord, our authority for living. Through his cruel death and glorious resurrection, Jesus paid the ultimate price to be our Savior, to forgive our sins, offer us eternal life, and establish the Church on an eternal foundation.

When we consider the great discomfort Jesus endured

to lead us to God, studying and seeking to appreciate opinions other than our own suddenly becomes a very small price to pay for the opportunity to help live out God's calling to love one another in the midst of profound disagreement.

Understanding views within United Methodism

Currently, there are three main theological positions in regards to LGBTQ inclusion within United Methodism:

- *The traditionalist view,*
- *The progressive view, and*
- *The centrist view.*

I will do my best to articulate each of these viewpoints in a charitable, authentically Christian manner. However, it needs to be acknowledged there is significant diversity in how those who hold these viewpoints would articulate them. No brief summary can do justice to this broad span of voices.

In fact, it is difficult to decide what to call these viewpoints, because each point of view has several descriptors frequently used to identify it. Within the following pages I have chosen "traditionalist" to refer to a viewpoint which is also referred to in places as conservative, evangelical, or orthodox.

"Progressive" is a term generally referring to groups that are also called liberal. "Centrist" views are labeled moderate in many contexts. I have chosen traditionalist, centrist, and progressive because they are terms each group frequently uses for the purposes of self-identification. Likewise, those with other viewpoints tend to use these terms in a respectful manner to refer to this differing point of view.

The traditionalist view

Traditionalists maintain the practice of homosexuality is contrary to the will of God. They tend to base this view primarily on the consistent witness of scripture, which they believe is supported by human life cycle patterns and studies of psychological health.

When considering the Biblical witness, traditionalists acknowledge the difficulty of discerning which Old Testament laws should be followed by Christians and which are no longer mandatory.

Based on the condemnations of homosexuality they find in the New Testament, traditionalists often interpret the Old Testament passages banning male homosexual practice in Leviticus 18:22 and Leviticus 20:13 as an indication that, from the very beginning, God did not intend for humanity to engage in same gender sexual relations.

Traditionalists also acknowledge that the instructions to put men caught in homosexual behavior to death in Leviticus 20:13 must be discarded just as many of the violent penalties for breaking religious laws in the Old Testament must be abandoned due to the example of Christ's gracious love for sinners.

Some traditionalists view the destruction of Sodom

and Gomorrah in Genesis 19 as a condemnation of homosexuality, while others maintain that Genesis 19 condemns
rape and sexual violence rather than homosexuality.

The core of the traditionalist understanding of basic
scriptural witness regarding homosexuality comes from
chapter 1 of Paul's letter to the Romans. In Romans 1:22-
28, Paul writes:

> 22 Although they claimed to be wise, they became
> fools 23 and exchanged the glory of the immortal God for
> images made to look like a mortal human being and birds
> and animals and reptiles.
> 24 Therefore God gave them over in the sinful desires of
> their hearts to sexual impurity for the degrading of their
> bodies with one another. 25 They exchanged the truth about
> God for a lie, and worshiped and served created things rather
> than the Creator—who is forever praised. Amen.
> 26 Because of this, God gave them over to shameful
> lusts. Even their women exchanged natural sexual relations
> for unnatural ones. 27 In the same way the men also aban-
> doned natural relations with women and were inflamed with
> lust for one another. Men committed shameful acts with
> other men, and received in themselves the due penalty for
> their error.
> 28 Furthermore, just as they did not think it worthwhile
> to retain the knowledge of God, so God gave them over to a
> depraved mind, so that they do what ought not to be done.
> (NIV)

Romans 1:26-27 is the only place in the Christian Bible
where female homosexuality is explicitly discussed. Using
this scripture, traditionalists interpret the primary problem with male or female homosexuality as being "unnatural" and out of line with God's intentions for humanity.

Many traditionalists would also view 1st Corinthians
6:9 and 1 Timothy 1:9-11 as including homosexual behavior in a list of actions contrary to God's will.

In regards to the specific teachings of Jesus, traditionalists note, when speaking of marriage in Matthew 19:4-6, Jesus quotes the book of Genesis in saying:

> 4 "Haven't you read," he replied, "that at the beginning the Creator 'made them male and female,' 5 and said, 'For this reason a man will leave his father and mother and be united to his wife, and the two will become one flesh'? 6 So they are no longer two, but one flesh. Therefore what God has joined together, let no one separate." (NIV)

To traditionalists, this teaching seems to presuppose Jesus' perspective that marriage was created solely for a man and woman.

Traditionalists find their views of scripture reinforced by their understandings of the natural world and human psychology. They often view the natural world as containing God's design for human flourishing. In examining humanity, it's not hard to see how males and females were created to produce life and to complement one another with their physical attributes and personality traits. Traditionalists point out same sex relationships are incapable of producing life through sexual interaction. Moreover, they could argue, basic biology indicates we are not designed to engage in sexually intimate acts with same sex partners.

Concerning psychological health, traditionalists might worry the current permissive guidelines of the American Psychological Association regarding lesbian, gay, and bisexual persons are overly influenced by a desire to be politically correct, failing to fully appreciate the psychological dangers of these lifestyles.

It is not uncommon for traditionalists to believe

many mental health experts with more conservative perspectives are being unfairly silenced and their research is going unfunded and unfairly discounted simply because it is out of line with the current ethos of American academia.

Traditionalists support their concerns by studies indicating those who engage in homosexual, bisexual, or transsexual lifestyles experience greater risks of depression, substance abuse, and suicide.

For these reasons, most traditionalists want to see the church articulate and uphold a traditional understanding of human sexuality in a compassionate manner.

The progressive view

Progressives tend to see human sexuality as a gift from God with diverse expressions. Many progressives view homosexuality, bisexuality, and transsexuality as sexual orientations intended within God's creative purposes.

The testimony of scripture, as understood from a progressive viewpoint, centers around Genesis 1:31, "God saw all that he had made, and it was very good." (NIV)

Since sexuality seems to be an orientation rather than a choice, progressives see homosexuality, bisexuality, and transsexuality as being included in this scripture.

Progressives consider the prohibitions on homosexuality in the Old Testament as outdated rules, based on a primitive understanding of human psychology. Just as Old Testament rules like Jewish dietary laws can be disregarded by Christians, restrictions related to sexual orientation no longer need to be followed by the vast majority of Christians.

While progressives acknowledge Jesus did not directly address sexual orientations other than heterosexuality in his teaching, they question why Jesus would not directly condemn other sexual orientations if they fell out of line with God's purposes for humanity.

From a progressive point of view, Jesus' affirmation of heterosexuality does not imply a corresponding condemnation of other orientations.

The lists of prohibitions found in 1 Corinthians and 1 Timothy are often interpreted in one of two ways by the progressive community. Some view these lists as expressing the culturally conditioned attitudes of the author, not the timeless truth of God. Others question whether the Greek words (malakoi and arsenokoitai) used in these epistles could more accurately be translated as "weak mindedness" rather than homosexual relations.

The core of the progressive critique of traditionalist understandings of the scriptural witness regarding sexuality can be found in the progressive interpretation of Romans 1:22-28. Progressives point out Paul condemned homosexual practice in verses 26-28 because it was unnatural. They further note Paul had no understanding of sexuality outside of heterosexuality as being a naturally occurring biological orientation. Therefore, since the dominant scientific views of our day now considers homosexuality to be an orientation, there is no longer reason to view it as being unnatural.

Following this line of thought, if homosexuality is

not unnatural, Paul's reason for condemning it becomes null and void. Paul's opinions in Romans 1:22-28 can best be interpreted as his own culturally conditioned opinion, rather than through the timeless truth of God.

In viewing the natural world, progressives remind us homosexuality is often experienced as being as natural to one person as heterosexuality is to another. While natural procreation is not possible among homosexual couples, progressives note the inability to produce children is not seen as a problematic factor in determining if a hetero- sexual couple should be together. Moreover, it could be noted mutual love and affection among same-sex couples and the care they give their children is quite life giving.

Concerning the psychological health implications of sexual orientations other than heterosexuality, progressives look to the standards of the American Psychological Asso- ciation (APA). The APA ceased classifying homosexuality as a mental disorder in the 1970s after studies done as early as the 1950s failed to show any problematic psychological differences between heterosexuals and homosexuals.

The APA now contends:

"The longstanding consensus of the behavioral and social sci- ences and the health and mental health professions is that homo- sexuality per se is a normal and positive variation of human sexual orientation."[1]

In accordance with these views, progressives want the church to be fully affirming of non-heterosexual orientations and relationships. They believe that the Christian mandate to work for social justice compels the

1 http://www.apa.org/about/policy/sexual-orientation.aspx

United Methodist Church to extend marriage ceremonies to non-heterosexual couples and to allow ordination for anyone called and equipped for ministry regardless of sexual orientation.

The centrist view

Within United Methodism, centrists are better defined by their hopes for resolving the conflict over human sexuality between traditionalists and progressives, rather than by a consistent theological perspective or opinion on Biblical interpretation. Centrists want to see the United Methodist Church reach a creative compromise, allowing both progressive and traditional expressions of United Methodism to co-exist within the same denomination.

Centrists often express their stance on the issue by sharing a famous quote which originated with Rupertus Meldenius, a 17th century German Lutheran, who later became associated with John Wesley:

> "In the essentials unity, in the non-essentials liberty, in all things charity."

From a centrist perspective, viewpoints concerning sexual orientation are important in regards to human health, but non-essential to the essence of Christianity and the mission of the church. With this in mind, they would like to see a method which allows progressive churches to formulate progressive policies, for traditionalist churches to have traditionalist policies, and for the denomination to shift its energies from the debate over human sexuality to the weightier matters of reaching out to the unchurched. In the centrist way of thinking, it is more important to deepen the faith of church members, start new churches, revitalize established churches, and work together to bring hope and healing to communities affected by killer diseases, rampant poverty, explicit bigotry and low social mobility.

Many centrists greatly appreciate both the traditional and progressive arguments surrounding human sexuality. Some have yet to make up their minds concerning the issues of sexual orientations and lifestyles, other than affirming heterosexuality is within God's creative intentions for humanity.

Other centrists might consider themselves to be traditionalists or progressives. However, their respect for those with whom they disagree leads them to seek a central path, allowing those of differing opinions to follow their consciences while remaining united as one denomination.

Another favorite quote of centrists actually did originate with John Wesley:

> "Though we cannot think alike, may we not love alike? May we not be of one heart, though we are not of one opinion?"

Within United Methodism, the centrist movement asks: May we not be of one denomination, though we are not of one opinion?

Diversity within viewpoints

While preparing to write this book, I spoke to numerous leaders, representing various viewpoints within

United Methodism. During these conversations, I was struck by the diversity of views regarding Biblical witness, scientific truth, and political hopes. I even noted different opinions among leaders who would identify themselves as being in the same camp.

I have summarized the traditionalist, progressive, and centrist positions. In so doing, I have necessarily left out a good bit of diversified opinion within those viewpoints. I have attempted to articulate the summaries of these basic views in a manner easily understandable and respectable to those who hold differing views.

There are some traditionalists who view the Bible and science as condemning non-heterosexual orientations more strongly than I may have described in this chapter. There are some progressives who believe the Bible contains thinly veiled homosexual relationships among some of its main characters, though I have chosen not to explore those passages.

There are significant differences of opinion among traditionalists regarding whether it is possible to remain united as a denomination, given the strength of the progressive minority within United Methodism.

There is also substantial diversity within the progressive camp, in regards to whether sexual orientations is biologically set or based upon life experiences and personal choices.

For the purpose of brevity we often talk about LGBTQ inclusion. It should be noted not everyone in the lesbian and gay community sees bi-sexuality or transsexuality as necessarily healthy. This argument works both ways. Just as there are among traditionalists, there are profound differences within the progressive movement over issues of sexuality.

Though the centrist camp has been largely defined by a desire to see the UMC remain unified, some in this group worry it might be too late. Many centrists remain fully committed, while others feel a gracious way out should be available for those traditionalists or progressives who no longer wish to co-exist within a big tent denomination. For these centrists, the primary focus of our denominational energies should move from debating sexuality to making disciples.

I hope this chapter has helped you appreciate the diversity of views among sincere faithful United Methodists. Perhaps it might even help you come to a greater appreciation of views other than your own.

In the midst of conflict over Biblical interpretation and scientific standards for discerning truth, it can be difficult to see a clear path forward. This conundrum reminds me of a Bible verse written for just such occasions.

In Psalm 119:105, it says:

"Your word is a lamp for my feet, a light on my path." (NIV)

Psalm 119 does not say God's word will provide daylight during the entire journey ahead. Instead God's word is more like a flashlight on a dark path. It gives us enough light to take the next step. The further we go, the more we learn to trust. Eventually, we develop faith this light will help us see where our next steps should be, even if we don't yet see the end of the road.

Chapter Three

Looking in the Mirror

Rediscovering Humility and Prevenient Grace

*"It was pride that changed angels into devils;
It is humility which makes men as angels."*

St. Augustine

For many of us, a powerful moment of hope and healing at the 2016 General Conference came on the second
day when Bishop Gregory V. Palmer called the UMC to
embrace humility. In making his appeal for humility
among the differing factions within United Methodism,
Palmer quoted St. Bernard of Clairvaux who, when asked
by his followers to list the four greatest virtues responded,
"humility, humility, humility, humility."

For Christians, humility requires us to:

- *not think of ourselves as inherently better or
  smarter than others;*
- *recognize that any truth we know is a gift we have
  acquired by God's grace;*
- *acknowledge how much we don't know;*

- *open our minds to the possibility God may choose to teach us truth through those with differing perspectives from our own; and*
- *accept the reality that we might see things very differently if we lived in a different context.*

Better than nobody

There's an old saying which goes something like this: "You're better than nobody, but nobody is better than you."

Regardless of who first coined this phrase, it reminds us of a fundamental truth: Deep down, we are all the same. None of us is better, more ethical, or inherently more valuable than anyone else.

This does not mean there is no such thing as the concept of right or wrong, or that all opinions are equal. It simply reminds us to treat everyone with respect and compassion because, if you were to walk a mile in their shoes, you might end up walking just like them.

We need this reminder in United Methodism. All of us are susceptible to biases. We develop biases based on height, weight, skin tone, hair, accent, profession, gender, nationality, disability, sexual orientation, political affiliation, religious affiliation, age and more. We even have biases towards people from different parts of our own towns, fans of opposing sports teams, and those who like different styles of music and clothing.

Sometimes these biases have deadly effects when one group dehumanizes another. Other times, the effects are much more benign and go unnoticed. In our best moments, working to move past harmful biases can lead to sacred experiences, allowing us a new ability to see God's handiwork in others who we might have overlooked or disregarded before.

One of our most common biases is to assume people who think like us are more intelligent, more realistic, more objective, and possess higher moral values than those who think differently. This was just as true in Jesus' day.

According to Matthew's Gospel, many Pharisees and Sadducees were coming to be baptized prior to Jesus' baptism by John the Baptist in the Jordan River. John, whose baptism was for the repentance of sins, surely realized that due to their religious heritage, the Pharisees and Sadducees did not feel they needed to be forgiven quite as much as everyone else. Rather than celebrate their presence, John's harsh challenge is recorded in Matthew, chapter 3:

> 7 "But when he saw many of the Pharisees and Sadducees coming to where he was baptizing, he said to them: "You brood of vipers! Who warned you to flee from the coming wrath? 8 Produce fruit in keeping with repentance. 9 And do not think you can say to yourselves, 'We have Abraham as our father.' I tell you that out of these stones God can raise up children for Abraham. 10 The ax is already at the root of the trees, and every tree that does not produce good fruit will be cut down and thrown into the fire.
> 11 "I baptize you with water for repentance. But after me comes one who is more powerful than I, whose sandals I am not worthy to carry. He will baptize you with the Holy Spirit and fire. 12 His winnowing fork is in his hand, and he will clear his threshing floor, gathering his wheat into the barn and burning up the chaff with unquenchable fire." (NIV)

Apparently, the Sadducees and Pharisees thought their lineage from Abraham made them more righteous than others. John the Baptist cuts through their pretension. He reminds them, in no uncertain terms, God could make children of Abraham from rocks on the ground.

We United Methodists have something in common with most other religious groups. We tend to judge ourselves as better able to discern the truth because of our open-minded theological perspective, beliefs regarding Biblical authority, the seminary we attended, or even the success of our local church.

It's easy to disregard the opinions of folks who don't think like us. We might find ourselves thinking:

"Those folks are still caught in the myth of objectivity propagated by enlightenment thinking;" or

"Can you believe how fundamentalist they are? I doubt they ask hard questions about the Bible or studied any real science;" or

"That perspective is just the residue of 1960s liberalism. That's what started our decline;" or

"They're from an underdeveloped country, we can't expect them to understand;" or

"That's nothing more than a Republican talking point;" or

"That's straight out of the Democratic party platform;" or

"Well, what would you expect from someone from that region of the country or that part of the world?"

Most of us would never say it out loud, but we think these thoughts silently while smiling and nodding our heads during conversations. Afterwards we excuse ourselves, often without exploring the origins of the opinions we have written off so quickly, then move back to the "smart" people who think like us.

Perhaps it's time to recognize God doesn't need our local church, our region, our country, our seminary, or our particular theological perspective to make faithful Christians. God can make faithful United Methodists out of pebbles on the ground. So instead of patting ourselves on the back for being so wise and faithful, perhaps we should put forth the effort to better understand the other faithful United Methodists in our midst.

It might be time for progressives to try to understand how compassionate, caring, open-minded, scientifically astute traditionalists could believe sexual orientations outside of heterosexuality are out of line with God's design. Maybe it's time for traditionalists to try to understand how progressives could value Biblical authority and a personal saving relationship with Jesus Christ experienced through the indwelling of the Holy Spirit while advocating for all God's children to be equally respected within the church.

Maybe it's time for centrists to stop seeing themselves as the adults in the room, charged with getting progressives and traditionalists to play nice together. Perhaps centrists should begin recognizing conflicts surrounding human sexuality are caused by profound differences over right and wrong that have life and death consequences.

'Tis mercy all

Embracing humility and viewing others as your

equals does not mean you believe all opinions are equally valid. It does mean you recognize any wisdom you have gained or truth you have discerned as a gift from God. You did not earn it. God gave you the opportunity to acquire it and you simply made yourself available to receive it.

James 1:17 tell us:

> Every good and perfect gift is from above, coming
> down from the Father of the heavenly lights, who does not
> change like shifting shadows. (NIV)

God is the giver of every perfect gift and all truth comes from God. Any truth we discern is largely based on the people who taught us and the life experiences that shaped us.

We should, therefore, be careful before taking pride in our wisdom. It is all a gift. God's prevenient grace surrounds us and endows us with the ability to reason and discern right and wrong, true and false, good and bad.

In Charles Wesley's unforgettable hymn, "And Can It Be That I Should Gain," he writes,

> 'Tis mystery all: th'Immortal dies:
> Who can explore His strange design?
> In vain the firstborn seraph tries
> To sound the depths of love divine.
> 'Tis mercy all! Let earth adore,
> Let angel minds inquire no more.

If Wesley was right to believe even angels cannot fully comprehend the truth of God, we should be quick to acknowledge any truth we comprehend as a gift from God.

Additionally, we should be equally quick to acknowledge the many reasons why other smart, intelligent, devoted Christians might see the issue differently than us.

The edge of the horizon

Having recognized our wisdom as a gift from God, the next step towards humility requires us to acknowledge how much we don't know.

Gazing into the horizon on a clear day, a person can see approximately 3.1 miles ahead before the curvature of the earth takes the rest out of sight. When you are running your first 5K race, 3.1 miles seems like a long way. Compared to the circumference of the earth, which is 24,901 miles, 3.1 miles doesn't seem quite so long after all.

Even if you were to look at the earth from an airplane flying at 35,000 feet on a perfectly clear day, you would only be able to see about 230 miles, meaning approximately 99 percent of the world would be entirely of out view.

When it comes to understanding the mysteries of God, we have been given a miraculous and trustworthy picture of God's nature and design for creation. We see this picture through the life, death, and resurrection of Jesus Christ; the witness of scripture; the teachings of the church; and the logic of reason. Still, when it comes to understanding the totality of God's essence and the depths of the great mysteries of life, we probably understand a minuscule amount on a good day.

Consider what God says to Job when Job contends God

has failed him. In Job 38, God begins by asking Job some tough questions.

> 4 "Where were you when I laid the earth's foundation?
> Tell me, if you understand.
> 5 Who marked off its dimensions? Surely you know!
> Who stretched a measuring line across it?
> 6 On what were its footings set,
> or who laid its cornerstone—
> 7 while the morning stars sang together
> and all the angels shouted for joy?"
> 8 "Who shut up the sea behind doors
> when it burst forth from the womb,
> 9 when I made the clouds its garment
> and wrapped it in thick darkness,
> 10 when I fixed limits for it
> and set its doors and bars in place,
> 11 when I said, 'This far you may come and no farther;
> here is where your proud waves halt'?" (NIV)

God continues to question Job about the many mysteries of creation throughout chapters 38 and 39, before finally concluding in Job 40:2, "Will the one who contends with the Almighty correct him?"(NIV)

Sometimes God seems to be harsh with Job in this conversation. However, I don't think God's intentions were harsh at all.

Instead, I hear God saying, "Job, have you forgotten how big I am? Have you forgotten how powerful I am? Do you think I am incapable of rescuing and restoring you? Job, do you remember I have the whole world, including you, in my hands? Job, I am not about to drop the world or let you slip out of my loving grasp."

When it comes to the United Methodist debate surrounding LGBTQ inclusion, how badly do we United

Methodists need to hear God say, "Where were you when I designed humanity? Where were you when I knit you together in your mother's womb in a fearful and wonderful manner?"

Sexuality is one of the great blessings and great mysteries of human life. Even with all we know about human sexuality, there is still much we don't know and may never know.

While we spend a lot of energy trying to make decisions regarding sexuality on behalf of the church, if you are honest would you even claim to understand your own sexuality completely? I wouldn't.

I know my sexuality is a gift from God, functioning as a blessing in my life when I express it within strict God-given limits. These limits begin with celibacy in singleness and faithfulness in marriage. They go on to include how I look at and respect women, what thoughts I allow in my head, and what images I allow to appear on my computer or TV screen, to name just a few.

Within these firm bounds, sexuality is a wonderful gift, bringing intimacy and joy. Outside these bounds, it brings confusion and pain. This is what I know about my own heterosexuality, but do I understand it fully? No way. Not even close.

Recognizing how much we do not know about our own sexuality, much less the sexuality of others, will not solve all our problems or make the solutions self-evident. What it can do is grant us the humility necessary to find new and loving ways to relate to one another in the midst of our differences.

Teachable moments

One of the sacred ways humility changes our relation-ships occurs when we learn to view our conversations as opportunities to learn, rather than chances to convince others. Any parent, teacher, or coach will tell you teach-able moments are as sacred as they are infrequent. When a teachable moment occurs, you have to be ready to take advantage because they do not happen all the time.

When a player makes a mistake in the big game, it's not the best time to criticize their attitude at practice that week. When a teenager is hangry (hungry + angry), it's not a good time to talk about their behavior towards their siblings. When a student fails a test, you do not immedi-ately go over everything they did wrong.

What any savvy parent, teacher, or coach would do in these situations would be to work through their cur-rent emotions in a supportive manner (feeding them, for instance), and then vigilantly watch for a teachable moment to present itself. The very best parents, teachers, and coaches are the ones who relate in ways that turn non-teachable moments into teachable moments.

You may have known someone who had this great talent. Someone who seemed to know just what to say to calm you down, take the pressure off, and to help you think more clearly.

What if we could learn to do this for those who don't think exactly like we do? What if our greatest hope in con-versations with those who disagree with us became the desire to learn more about their perspective, rather than

62

get the last word? What if we all learned to approach difficult conversations about LGBTQ inclusion within United
Methodism in a manner that would help, instead of harm,
build up, rather than tear down? I believe we can.

A shepherd mentors a head of state

The Bible gives us an example of just such a conversation in Exodus 18 when Moses finds himself teetering
on the brink of his leadership capacity and talks to his
father-in-law, Jethro, about his predicament.

At this point Moses has publicly defied Pharaoh,
defeated the most powerful army on earth, and led the
Hebrews out of slavery towards the Promised Land. God
has spoken directly to Moses on numerous occasions and
performed mind boggling miracles through him.

Not surprisingly, Moses' reunion with his shepherd-
ing father-in-law begins as we might expect, with Jethro
congratulating Moses and praising God for all that has
taken place.

That's when the story takes an unexpected turn. As
Jethro observes Moses' daily practice of settling disputes
between Hebrews, he recognizes some serious deficien-
cies in Moses' leadership style. Without Moses asking,
Jethro takes it upon himself to tell Moses what he needs
to do. Listen to how forceful Jethro speaks to his son-in-
law in Exodus 18:

> 17 Moses' father-in-law replied, "What you are doing is
> not good. 18 You and these people who come to you will only
> wear yourselves out. The work is too heavy for you; you
> cannot handle it alone. 19 Listen now to me and I will give

you some advice, and may God be with you. You must be the people's representative before God and bring their disputes to him. 20 Teach them his decrees and instructions, and show them the way they are to live and how they are to behave. 21 But select capable men from all the people—men who fear God, trustworthy men who hate dishonest gain— and appoint them as officials over thousands, hundreds, fifties and tens. 22 Have them serve as judges for the people at all times, but have them bring every difficult case to you; the simple cases they can decide themselves. That will make your load lighter, because they will share it with you. 23 If you do this and God so commands, you will be able to stand the strain, and all these people will go home satisfied."

24 Moses listened to his father-in-law and did everything he said. (NIV)

The most amazing thing about this story is not that Jethro, a nomadic shepherd, provides invaluable leadership counsel to one of the greatest leaders the world has ever known. It is when Moses listens to Jethro and heeds his advice.

Imagine how tempting it must have been for Moses to disregard Jethro's advice. Moses might well have thought to himself, "Now listen here, you uneducated shepherd. I appreciate that fact you let me marry your daughter and showed me the ropes when it came to taking care of sheep, but you are in way over your head. I was educated in Pharaoh's palace and I have spoken directly to God.

"I think I know a little more about being a head of state than you. Just because I'm your son-in-law, you think you can tell me what to do? What could I possibly learn from you? All you've ever done was learn to herd a couple hundred sheep, I'm leading hundreds of thousands of people."

Thankfully, Moses never acted upon those thoughts if he had them. He considered Jethro's advice for what it was worth and implemented his advice in its entirety.

Moses delegated responsibility, mentored a new generation of leaders, and created a more sustainable pattern of living, allowing him to remain leader of the Hebrews for the rest of his life.

Imagine what could have happened if Moses had failed to take Jethro's advice. Burn out, poor decision making, health problems, an early death and an uncertain future would have surely faced the Hebrews who followed him. Instead, Moses led faithfully until the end of his days and left the Hebrews well prepared to enter the Promised Land.

All this happened because one of the greatest leaders in history was humble enough to take advice from a savvy old shepherd who lived in the wilderness.

If we as United Methodists could cultivate even a fraction of the humility Moses possessed, it might allow us to discover an important lesson. By learning from those with diverse perspectives, we learn how to better minister to the communities they represent. Without such humility, our diversity will continue to be a constant source of conflict, diverting our most precious resources from the communities to which we are called to minister.

The water in which we swim

In addition to allowing us to learn from one another,

humility enables us to recognize how much our own opinions are shaped by the environment in which we were raised and in which we live as adults.

If you put a fish in a small aquarium, the fish will remain small no matter how much you feed it. If you put a fish in the ocean, it will grow as large as its diet allows. The water in which we swim has a lot to do with what we become.

In the Appalachian region of the country I call home, we pride ourselves on the fact our region of the Confederacy had large numbers of Union sympathizers during the Civil War who opposed the war and the institution of slavery.

Why was this? Was it because we had more highly developed moral consciences, allowing us to clearly see the intolerable nature of slavery? Was it because our more enlightened minds were naturally less prone to racism?

No. It was because our mountainous terrain and peculiar climate did not lend itself to cotton farming and we did not want to die in a war so other people could get rich raising cotton with slaves.

Where we live and the mainstream patterns of thinking in our communities shape us more than we like to admit. The same was true in Biblical times.

Consider the early church debates on circumcision contained in Acts 15. Many Jewish Christians in Jerusalem could not understand how anyone could be saved apart from circumcision. Paul and Barnabas, who had seen God's work among the Gentiles, felt quite differently.

Thankfully, Paul and Barnabas' argument won the day and I do not have to have sensitive conversations about a small surgical procedure before I accept men into membership at our church.

If you were a Jewish Christian in Jerusalem at this time, you probably would have felt strong feelings about the issue. If you were a Jewish Christian living elsewhere in the Roman world, you might have had a different opinion. If you were a Gentile woman, you likely would have had yet another opinion, and if you were a Gentile man, you probably would have the strongest opinion of all.

When it comes to the United Methodist debate on LGBTQ inclusion, the dominant cultural attitudes of our region, our family, and our local church have a lot to do with why we think the way we do.

During the 2016 General Conference, there was a session in which delegates were encouraged to switch tables and engage in dialogue surrounding LGBTQ inclusion with those from different regions. An engaging pastor from the Western Jurisdiction sat at my table. He described himself as somewhere between moderate and conservative on the theological spectrum and went on to share that many of the more progressive members of his delegation would consider him extremely conservative.

As he shared his views on LGBTQ inclusion, however, it became apparent in this matter his opinions were just as progressive as the views of the self-described "progressives" in our delegation from the southeastern jurisdiction. Apparently, what it means to be progressive or conservative or moderate depends on where you live.

This conversation reminded me no matter what we consider ourselves, it helps to remember our view might be different if we lived in a different region of the United States or in a different part of the world.

Recognizing the extent to which our environment shapes our thinking has led many United Methodists to propose "local options" for solving the divide over LGBTQ inclusion. These proposed local options have included policies such as:

- *Making the United States a central conference with the right to set its own policies in this regard.*
- *Putting the decision-making power into the hands of the jurisdictions and central conferences.*
- *Allowing local churches, annual conferences, and pastors to decide how to handle the issues.*

In each instance, however, these local option proposals have been soundly defeated and already there are traditionalist and progressive groups claiming any local option proposed by the special commission would be a deal breaker.

If you find yourself fearful of any local option for LGBTQ inclusion, I would ask you to consider your reasons why you feel this way. Is it because you cannot recognize a Christian who believes differently than you regarding LGBTQ inclusion as a faithful United Methodist, or is it because you fear compromise on these issues would eventually lead to the ability of more localized denominational bodies to rewrite the basic historical theological tenets of Christianity and the Wesleyan understandings of grace holding us together?

Could it be you feel any deviation from your personal position, be it traditionalist or progressive, would constitute a basic human rights violation by the UMC which would do more harm than a denominational schism?

On the other hand, if you find yourself extremely fearful of schism and willing to make almost any compromise to prevent one, I would ask you to consider these questions:

- *What is it that you believe holds us together as United Methodists?*
- *Is there a way for us to move forward together that does not compromise our basic beliefs and allows us to focus our energies on sharing the Gospel rather than denominational infighting?*

Finally, regardless of how you would personally answer the questions above regarding the local option and schism, can you look at those who think differently than you and understand that if you walked in their shoes you might think exactly like they do?

The great difficulty our denomination is experiencing as we seek to find a way forward through the conflict over LGBTQ inclusion comes largely from our United Methodist commitment to be a connectional church with centralized beliefs and policies.

In the next two chapters, we will turn our attention to the current state of connectionalism within United

Methodism and changes necessary if we hope to live out Wesley's vision of spreading scriptural holiness.

Chapter Four

Embracing Diversity

Our Open Table

*A faith-based perspective . . . creates room for
the Holy Spirit to work in marvelous ways.*

I squirmed when a Bible study participant said, "What
I like about the United Methodist Church is since we are
not a creedal church, we can pretty much believe whatever we want."

My reaction must have been very noticeable because
the person who said it immediately looked at me and said,
"Isn't that right, pastor?"

Imagine the surprise when I shared the United Methodist Church officially subscribes to 43 detailed "Articles
of Religion" containing our basic theological doctrines
which are much more nuanced than any of the ancient or
modern creeds. Additionally, we expect our members to
subscribe to a strictly structured style of church governance. To say we are not a creedal church means we allow
those who have found a saving relationship with Jesus

Christ to join our fellowship before they have had time to study every line of a particular creed with microscopic precision. It doesn't mean we do not have formal beliefs about the nature of God and the Church.

Over the past two centuries, our beliefs and policies have allowed our denomination to embrace diverse perspectives with American Christianity and diverse segments of the world population. Part of the current conflict within our denomination stems from one of our great strengths: We are a denomination which welcomes diverse Christians into its fellowship.

We've enabled people with very different social views to worship and serve together, to cry at funerals and clap at weddings beside each other, and to form life-long friendships rooted in an allegiance to Christ that supersedes our differing opinions.

In our recent past, the term "connectionalism" has become the phrase we use to express how, as Christians with diverse views, we are connected to one another as United Methodists through our shared beliefs and policies. Whether diversity remains a strength or becomes a stumbling block for United Methodism in the future depends largely on how we understand and practice our connectionalism going forward.

Within any community, political or ecclesial, diversity can be a great asset or it can lead to polarization, segregation, and in the worst instances, violence. Without a shared understanding of what unites us, diversity leads to harm. With a strong unified identity, diversity blesses us all.

Thankfully, history provides us with a number of communities, both ancient and modern, who changed the world by discovering a unified foundation strong enough to knit together extremely diverse constituencies.

A strange band of brothers (and sisters)

> 12 One of those days Jesus went out to a mountainside to pray, and spent the night praying to God. 13 When morning came, he called his disciples to him and chose twelve of them, whom he also designated apostles: 14 Simon (whom he named Peter), his brother Andrew, James, John, Philip, Bartholomew, 15 Matthew, Thomas, James son of Alphaeus, Simon who was called the Zealot, 16 Judas son of James, and Judas Iscariot, who became a traitor. (Luke 6:12-16, NIV)

Jesus' twelve disciples were an odd bunch. Some were fishermen and tradesmen, the kind of blue collar workers you would expect to hang out with a carpenter like Jesus. Then there was Matthew, a tax collector. To those in Jesus' time, he would have been considered a Jew who sold his soul to Rome. He was known as a scoundrel who cheated his fellow Jews out of hard earned money so he could be moderately wealthy.

There was also Simon the Zealot, a revolutionary who would do anything to expel the Roman occupiers out of the Promised Land, even if it meant embracing terrorist tactics and conspiring to carry out well-planned assassinations.

From the outside, we would expect all the other disciples to despise Matthew and Simon. Why should they tolerate someone who would betray his own religion and tribe by cozying up to the enemy to earn a little extra cash? It stands to reason many of the disciples may have been concerned Simon would start a fight and get them all killed.

The diversity of Jesus' disciples becomes even more astounding when we look beyond these twelve men. You will notice that Luke 6:13 says "he called his disciples to him and chose twelve of them." (NIV)

The twelve who became apostles were always a part of a larger band of Jesus' disciples. This larger group of disciples was more than a strange band of brothers. It was a strange band of brothers and sisters; making Jesus the only ancient Jewish rabbi on record to have female disciples.

What could possibly hold such a diverse group of disciples together? One thing: They were all Messianic Jews who believed the One True God, the God of Israel, had sent Jesus to be the Messiah.

The diversity of Jesus' followers did not stop with his death. It exploded. A few decades after Jesus death, a former Jewish leader named Paul, having made a name for himself first by persecuting Christians and then by becoming a Christian himself, would write: "There is neither Jew nor Gentile, neither slave nor free, nor is there male and female, for you are all one in Christ Jesus." (Galatians 3:28, NIV)

What kind of community could possibly contain Jews and Gentiles united as one people? Where in the world could slaves and free people come together as equals? What place was there in the ancient patriarchal society where women were respected as much as their male counterparts? Answer: The early church.

The common foundation for this diverse world-changing community was the belief, after his death, Jesus had been resurrected and walked again on Earth, the experience of death and resurrection with him through baptism and their commitment to sharing Holy Communion together.

Jewish Christians began sending out missionaries to bless and teach Gentile Christian communities. Conversely, Gentiles Christians began taking up offerings to bless impoverished Jewish Christian communities. Women became leaders as churches began meeting in their homes and masters were taught to look at their slaves not as servants but as brothers. The diverse members of the early church undermined the power-hungry Roman culture through their compassionate living in a way that no revolutionary army ever could.

Companies without countries

Today, multinational corporations are reshaping our world. Some would say these companies are great assets. Others consider their contributions more ambiguous or even negative. No one questions their power to fundamentally restructure the world economy and many of the cultures within it.

Many major corporations spend vast resources on recruiting diverse workforces and providing cultural sensitivity training for their workers. They seek to unify their diverse employees through a shared commitment to the core values of the company, their own unique work-place culture, and a commitment to improve the bottom line.

Why would these hard-charging companies spend millions, perhaps even billions of dollars, to become more diverse? The answer is simple. They function within a competitive environment and have discovered diverse teams perform better than homogeneous teams.

In fact, if you were to place four extremely high performing individuals with similar backgrounds and perspectives on a team, then ask them to compete against a team of four individuals known for producing average results whose backgrounds and basic assumptions vary widely, in most cases the diverse team of average employees would consistently outperform the more homogeneous team of high performers.

Diverse teams are able to see challenges from many different points of view and choose the solutions best suited for the unique situation at hand. They uncover unspoken assumptions and test their accuracy rather than taking them for granted. While diverse teams may not be comprised of individual all-stars, together they are capable of achieving greatness.

As companies often have discovered the hard way, diversity does not guarantee greatness. It simply makes it possible. Whether or not a diverse team lives up to its potential depends greatly on whether they can unite around common values, goals, and cultural norms within their workplace. The great challenge of our time within the UMC is to discern whether we have common values, goals, and cultural norms uniting us to such a degree that our diversity becomes a strength rather than a source of hurtful conflict.

Eclectic dinner companions

One of the most effective ways the UMC recruits diverse constituents is through our practice of receiving Holy Communion. Before someone goes forward to partake of the bread and wine in a United Methodist Church, the pastor will generally say something to the effect of: "Anyone willing to repent of their sin and acknowledge their need of Jesus Christ and his grace is welcome to come to his table."

We do not require communion participants to be members of any church, much less our own. They do not have to be baptized, nor do they have to be able to recount a conversion experience where their heart was strangely warmed. They simply have to love Christ, repent of their sins, and seek to live in peace with their neighbors.

When I was in seminary, it was intellectually fashionable to point out that John Wesley might never have intended for the unbaptized to come to the Lord's Table. It's true: He called communion a "converting ordinance," but it may well have been in the day and time he lived, with an established national church in which infant baptism was the norm, he took it for granted everyone who would consider coming to the table would have already been baptized.

He could have called communion a "converting ordinance" in reference to those who had been baptized but had not yet personally accepted Christ as their Lord and Savior when they came to the table.

Eventually, the denomination could no longer ignore this possibility. A commission was formed to consider the theological foundations and current practices within our church regarding the celebration of Holy Communion. What we discovered was, while we could not be sure of John Wesley's exact position on the matter, the position of United Methodists was crystal clear. Over the centuries the open table had become one of the primary unifying means of grace within local United Methodist churches.

Our United Methodist identity has been formed to such a degree by the open table that it would be hard for many of our members to still feel as if they were United Methodist at all if the table was closed. In the open table, we hear Christ's evangelistic call to come as we are, without pretense, relying on His grace to cleanse us and save us. In the open table, we find we are all equals because we sit beside each other. There is only one host at the table. We are guests.

The open table gives us a glimpse of the heavenly kingdom and makes us distinctively United Methodist. Other traditions have beautiful communion liturgies and theologies we respect. But the open table not only reminds us of our communion theology, it reminds us of our calling as Methodists to spread scriptural holiness and welcome the lost and forgotten into Christian fellowship. The open table humbles us as we come made worthy to receive communion only by Christ's invitation.

In many ways, it is the open table that makes diversity such a cherished attribute within United Methodism and gives power to the vision of United Methodism as a big tent church, big enough for traditionalists, progressives, and everyone in between. Big enough for anyone who loves Christ, repents of their sins, and seeks to live in peace.

Arguments at the dinner table

I suspect just about every family occasionally gets into arguments at the dinner table. The dinner table, as it turns out, is a marvelous place for families to work through their differences. So long as everyone at the table shares mutual love for one another, along with a willingness to sacrifice for the good of the family, most disputes can be dealt with in a loving and constructive manner that strengthens the unity of the family.

The arguments threatening the unity of United Methodists who have been called to share at Christ's open table have not centered on our 43 Articles of Religion. No substantial proposal to change our foundational theological doctrine has reached the General Conference in quite some time. The current argument revolves around our Social Principles, which appear soon after the Articles of Religion in The Book of Discipline.

According to The Book of Discipline, The Social Principles are not church law. Rather, they represent the best attempt of the General Conference to address current issues through the lens of our United Methodist beliefs.[1]

While we respect the Social Principles as constituting the accumulated wisdom of our spiritual forbearers and expressing the official position of the United Methodist Church, we do not hold them to be infallible or eternally unchanging. We understand we will never achieve the ability to fully apply the eternal truths of God to the complicated world in which we live with complete faithfulness. The Social Principles are simply our best efforts to envision how our world can more closely resemble the Kingdom of God.

Since the Social Principles are not church law, no local church, annual conference, pastor, or church member is obligated to personally subscribe to all of them. Pastors and lay persons have always been free to challenge and speak against the social principles they believe need to be changed, so long as they do not break church law in the process.

As the conflict over the Social Principles on LGBTQ inclusion has become heated, many progressive leaders have chosen to break church law in their attempt to undermine laws they consider unjust and discriminatory. At the same time, some traditionalist leaders have called for churches to stop paying denominational apportionments as a protest against those within our connection who openly violate church law.

These actions and the rhetoric that accompanies

---

1   The Book of Discipline of the United Methodist Church, 2016. p.105.

them have fractured the covenant relationship that holds us together and forced us to acknowledge that diversity, which has been one of our greatest assets, has now become one of our greatest challenges.

We must ask ourselves: Does our diversity leads us to hurt one another or enable us to be a healing witness within a hurting world? Our answer to this question has everything to do with whether we approach our diversity with a spirit of fear or a spirit of faith.

If we approach diversity with fear, we will reach a predictable outcome. We will continue to accuse those who see things differently as ruining our denomination. We will befriend and dialogue with only those who agree with us. We will think of those with different viewpoints as something less than Christian, and less than intelligent. We will approach all denomination decisions with the intent to acquire the maximum amount of power for those who share our point of view. With fear guiding us, a schism is not only probable, it is assured.

A faith based perspective, however, creates room for the Holy Spirit to work in marvelous ways. With the strength of faith, we can invite our diverse United Methodist brothers and sisters to join us at the table and have long overdue discussions that have been neglected while we fearfully fought against one another for power.

First, we need open discussions between traditionalists, centrists, and progressives concerning our articles of faith. Can we all still subscribe to them? Do we all still believe Jesus was actually raised from the dead? Is there still consensus that we are justified in God's sight solely by the work of Christ? Can we all accept the Holy Bible as the primary source for our theological beliefs and ethical standards?

Or are there even deeper differences within our fellowship that our arguments about LGBTQ inclusions have masked? Can we still find unity of belief in our Articles of Religion?

If indeed we discover our Articles of Religion can no longer hold us together within a shared theology, then schism may be desirable. A house united against itself cannot stand.

On the other hand, if we can firmly unite around our Articles of Religion, then we can turn our attention to the question of whether we can find sufficient respect for one another through our shared Articles of Religion to remain together in effective ministry without harming each other. Can we find creative solutions which would enable us to be united in a manner that does not violate the conscience of any and allows us to share Christ with all?

In the next chapter we will consider the internal and external barriers to sharing Christ for United Methodist churches in the 21st century.

If we have drifted so far apart from one another in our beliefs and practices we cannot remain one denomination, the open table will serve as a reminder that one day we will be rejoined around Christ's table at the heavenly banquet. If we remain united, the open table will provide an example of our unity within our diversity. In either scenario it's imperative we pray the best for those of other viewpoints and their churches.

I have always believed schism to be a sin. This belief has not changed. If anything, it has grown. It's a hard pill to swallow, but perhaps schism would be preferable to living together in an arrangement that causes us to continually hurt one another and fail to share Christ with our world.

Chapter Five

Getting Serious
About Connectionalism

*The grass isn't greener because it's on the other side of
the fence. The grass is greener where it is watered.*

When I bought my first house, I immediately noticed
the grass in my neighbor's yard looked much greener and
thicker than mine. So one fall afternoon, as my neighbor
and I were leaning against his fence and bemoaning the
state of our golf games, I switched the subject to his lush
grass. Thankfully, he was quick to share his secrets. He
explained how to make sure the soil has the proper nutrients, what type of seed to use, and when to seed the yard.

That fall, winter, and early spring I did exactly as he
had told me and by the first days of May, you could barely
tell the difference between our lawns. They were each full
and green and we were both quite proud. By the end of
the summer, however, things were back to the way they
had been. His lawn was beautiful. Mine was filled with
weeds and dirt patches.

I wondered what was wrong with my property. Was the soil on my land inferior to the soil just a few yards away in his yard? Did the slope of my property and lack of shade prohibit me from being able to grow a nice lawn?

None of these explanations made sense, so I asked my neighbor again. It turns out the difference was simple.

"Wil," he said. "You can put out all the seed and nutrients you want, but when it gets hot and dry you still have to water the lawn."

I learned more from my neighbor that day than just how to take care of my yard. I learned a good life lesson: The grass isn't greener because it's on the other side of the fence. The grass is greener where it is watered.

Preparing for the challenges ahead

Some within United Methodism seem to think if the UMC would just make the correct decision regarding LGBTQ inclusion and put a stop to all further debates, we would suddenly see established churches revitalized, new churches springing up faster than the weeds in my old yard, and 48 years of denominational decline in the United States reversed.

I wish it was this easy. Sure the grass looks greener on the other side of our current divide, but as soon as we get past this issue, there will be plenty of other dilemmas waiting for us, and they also have the potential to derail our mission of making disciples. Regardless of how our denomination handles LGBTQ inclusion, we are facing major challenges which will require us to muster all the wisdom, courage, and resources we can find.

Once again, when we look to scripture, it is quickly apparent we are not the only people to have encountered such a problem. Thankfully, the consistent witness of our spiritual ancestors reminds us the grass may not be greener on the other side of the fence, but God has more than enough water to make deserts into luscious gardens.

Between a rock and a dry place

Just a few months after the Israelite people were led out of Egypt through the Red Sea in the most inexplicably miraculous escape in history, they lost faith in God to provide for them. As they came to the wilderness of Sin, their food supply began to run short, so they complained to Moses:

> "If only we had died by the Lord's hand in Egypt! There we sat around pots of meat and ate all the food we wanted, but you have brought us out into this desert to starve this entire assembly to death." (Exodus 16:3, NIV)

It seems while they were slaves in Egypt, the Israelites believed the grass was greener in the wilderness. Most likely, many of them imagined once they were free from slavery under Pharaoh, everything would be wine and roses. Instead, as soon as they encountered their first real hardship, they looked back wistfully at the green grass of the Egyptian slave fields and wondered why they went to the trouble to escape in the first place.

You may remember God's response. God sends bread

from heaven, covering the ground with manna each morning. The Israelites could eat as much as they wanted during the day, but couldn't save any for the next day. God would give them more the next morning, so they would learn to trust God to provide each day. Then, to make sure they did not complain about a vegetarian diet, God also sent flocks of quails to their camp each evening, providing precious protein for the wandering people.

As the people journeyed past the wilderness of Sin, they came to a place known as Rephidim, where it was difficult to find drinking water. Let's consider, for a moment, how they responded to this challenge. Just imagine what the people had experienced within the previous 12 months.

They witnessed God bring plague after plague upon the Egyptians. They watched as Pharaoh allowed them to leave with many of his riches in tow. After Pharaoh changed his mind, they found themselves caught between the quickly advancing Egyptian army and the waters of the Red Sea.

While contemplating which would be less painful, to drown or die by sword, God parts the waters of the Red Sea, allowing them to cross to the other side. Having arrived safely on the opposite shore, the waters rush back together, drowning the world's most advanced fighting force in the process. A raucous celebration followed and the Hebrews continued their journey.

Soon they experience bitter drinking water, which God miraculously sweetens, and a food shortage, which God miraculously fixes by providing more bread and quail than they could ever eat.

Now, what do you imagine they did when they again had a hard time finding drinking water?

You guessed it: They decided the grass was greener back in Egypt.

Exodus 17:1-7 records their attitude and God's response.

> 1The whole Israelite community set out from the Desert of Sin, traveling from place to place as the Lord commanded. They camped at Rephidim, but there was no water for the people to drink. 2 So they quarreled with Moses and said, "Give us water to drink."
>
> Moses replied, "Why do you quarrel with me? Why do you put the Lord to the test?"
>
> 3 But the people were thirsty for water there, and they grumbled against Moses. They said, "Why did you bring us up out of Egypt to make us and our children and livestock die of thirst?"
>
> 4 Then Moses cried out to the Lord, "What am I to do with these people? They are almost ready to stone me."
>
> 5 The Lord answered Moses, "Go out in front of the people. Take with you some of the elders of Israel and take in your hand the staff with which you struck the Nile, and go. 6 I will stand there before you by the rock at Horeb. Strike the rock, and water will come out of it for the people to drink." So Moses did this in the sight of the elders of Israel. 7 And he called the place Massah and Meribah because the Israelites quarreled and because they tested the Lord saying, "Is the Lord among us or not?" (NIV)

How could the Hebrew's faith falter every time they encountered a challenge, especially considering all God had done for them? Could they not trust God to provide what they needed after God proved to be more than powerful enough for any problem they might face?

I have to admit it is hard for me to understand the weakness of the Hebrew's faith from an objective point of view. Well, that is, until I consider the weakness of my own.

God has always been there for me. In times of loss and confusion, God has never deserted me. God has given me blessings beyond my wildest imaginings in the form of work I love, a family I adore, and a prayer life that has led me to heights of joy and peace which defy description.

Yet, what happens when my life takes an unwanted turn? I often ask myself why God is allowing this to happen. If I cannot find a satisfactory answer to this question quickly enough, I move on to more dangerous questions:

- *Is God there at all?*
- *Are all those blessings I attribute to God actually just happy coincidences and wishful thinking?*

Since I struggle with these questions as a 21st century person living in a highly-developed nation with a loving family, a stable income, and a warm home, perhaps I should cut a little slack to the ancient Hebrews, who left everything they had ever known to journey through the wilderness to a place they had never seen. And, since I struggle with these same questions, perhaps I may be able to understand a little about the struggles of the Hebrews.

Maybe the real problem with the Hebrews and with me is not a lack of faith. It's the unrealistic expectations which spring from a "grass is greener" mentality. Could it be, when life is hard, I struggle to find blessings and, when failure comes calling, I struggle to understand why?

If the Hebrews were anything like me, they most likely heard about a promised land and imagined a four-day trip through the wilderness. It was nothing more than a long weekend. Who would have imagined a 40-year journey?

Nor would it surprise me if, when they heard about a land flowing with milk and honey, they failed to consider that bees and bears tend to hang out around such places and cattle do not get up at the crack of dawn to milk themselves.

For United Methodists in the United States and many countries throughout our world, we are facing the challenge of changing cultures. This challenge will necessitate many changes in how we practice our connectionalism, if we are to move from the wilderness of decline and division to the promised land of vibrancy and vitality.

At best, resolving our differences over LGBTQ inclusion, whether through compromise and unity or amicable division, will only allow us to focus on the challenges of the present. It will not guarantee an easy path ahead.

From brand churches to boutique churches

Several years ago, I began intentionally encouraging my congregants to go to church while they were out of town on vacation. This emphasis led many of them to report about their experiences while worshiping away from home.

As I reflected on their stories, I was struck at how many of our long-time members took great comfort in knowing they could often find a United Methodist church far from home that looked and felt a lot like their home church. They often found similar architecture, the same order of worship, the same style of music, and the same warm fellowship. In one case, a member even brought me a picture of a church, leading me to do a double-take. It looked exactly like our church. I was convinced this was a big joke and I was being shown a picture of our sanctuary until I noticed a small detail about the altar rail different from the rail of our altar.

The Methodist movement grew like wildfire on the American frontier in the 1800s, due largely to a common set of practices, beliefs, and policies established by the circuit riders in churches they launched and developed. The practices which enabled this explosive growth grew from a uniquely Methodist understanding of grace and of the American frontier culture, a culture more mobile and homogeneous, as well as much more British than the culture of the United States today.

As Methodism developed, the ability to print and distribute curriculum nationwide, along with the establishment of official educational requirements in Methodist seminaries, caused many of our Methodist churches in the Midwest to look and feel like our churches in the South. Not surprisingly, Southern Methodist churches looked and felt like Methodist churches in the Northeast, which looked at felt a lot like churches in the Northwest. Aside from the preachers' accents, there was little difference.

Pastors in those days were known for their willingness to move their families every year or two and were expected to be able to be effective wherever their moves took them. Bishops often worried if they left a pastor in one place too long, their messages would get stale. It was felt people needed to hear new perspectives every 12 to 24 months.

As the United States began to develop industrially, this way of thinking was further encouraged by the advent of the assembly line. Any worker, it was believed, should be able to plug into any part an assembly line as if no change had taken place.

This way of organizing churches created homogeneous churches which ministered very effectively to a society dominated by whites of British descent. As the United States continued to grow more ethnically and racially diverse, however, the Methodist way of raising up homogeneous churches with distinctly British cultures became less and less fruitful.

When I entered seminary in 2001, the United States had 40 demographic cultural groups, as defined by social demographers. These are groups of people who may or may not speak the same language or be from the same country of origin, but share basic assumptions about what they want out of life and what motivates them. They agree on things like what bothers them, what kind of products they want to buy, and how they like to communicate and receive communication. When I checked recently, the United States now had 71 defined demographic cultural groups.[1]

Though more rare than it used to be, I'm still sometimes seen by many as a young pastor. I suspect this is why I'm often asked in church settings how I think the

1   Mosaic USA. Group and Segment Descriptions. Experion Marketing Services, 2013. MissionInsite.com

church needs to change to reach a more diverse culture. To emphasis the seriousness of paying attention to our changing culture, I generally respond with something like, "How should I know? Way back when I went to seminary, our country was only about half as diverse as it is today."

In the hotel business, there is a fundamental distinction between brand hotels and boutique hotels. A brand hotel is a chain of hotels like Holiday Inn Express or Hilton Garden Inn. These hotels are designed to give you similar room features, similar levels of customer care and cleanliness, and similar interior designs. Brand hotels create a high level of customer loyalty by delivering a predicable experience and a consistent level of comfort.

Boutique hotels, on the other hand, specialize in offering an experience you cannot find anywhere else. Their architecture and design are unique and fit perfectly into the history of their community. Their room layouts, customer care practices, and amenities are all focused on helping you appreciate a unique aspect of the local culture.

When the United States had a more homogeneous culture, brand churches worked well for Methodism. People could trust wherever they went, they could get a familiar experience in the local United Methodist Church. Today, as our culture has become more diverse, denominational loyalty has become increasingly rare.

In the 21st century, United Methodism will need to evolve from its current structure as a group of brand churches to a denomination of increasingly boutique churches in style and function by sharing the Gospel with their community in a manner that remains distinctly Methodist in content, while becoming unique in cultural style.

Speaking in the vernacular

One of the great gifts evangelical Protestantism has given to the world is its commitment to communicate in the language of the people. While other religions, including some Christian denominations, have an official sacred language, evangelical Protestantism correctly recognizes the truth of Christ which transcends race, ethnicity, and language.

In the early days of Protestantism, martyrs gave their lives to translate the Bible out of Latin into languages the people could understand. In more recent years, the continued growth of Protestantism has been made possible by a commitment to sharing the Gospel in the linguistic and cultural vernacular language of the people.

While United Methodism displays a strong commitment to speaking in the linguistic and cultural vernacular of its people throughout the world, the same cannot always be said about our ministry within the United States.

When I first arrived as pastor in a small town in Southwest Virginia near the Appalachian coalfields, I took note of the other churches which were thriving in the area. I noticed all the thriving churches had one thing in common: Either their pastors were from the region or they had lived in the area for decades.

Needless to say, most Roman Catholic and mainline Protestant churches in the area were declining and struggling to keep their doors open, while Baptist churches, nondenominational, and Pentecostal churches were thriving. As I got to know the other pastors and their churches, I realized it was not theology which made the difference, because all the churches I became acquainted with preached a biblically and doctrinally robust understanding of Christianity.

Most of the mainline and Roman Catholic pastors were not from Southwest Virginia. They had lived the majority of their lives elsewhere and had been educated at seminaries in major cities, lacking appreciation for the Appalachian culture and the coal culture. These two cultures combined to give this region its distinctive ethos.

To complicate the matter further, these pastors rarely stayed at a church longer than 10 years. Armed with this insight, I immediately began trying to learn how to speak in small town Southwestern Virginia cultural vernacular. It wasn't until I learned to speak like everyone else that a truly transformational ministry began to happen at our church.

Within United Methodist appointment making, it is no longer enough to match a church to a pastor based on salary and years of experience. Using these categories as the primary criteria reflects assembly line thinking which no longer works in a diverse society.

When making appointments, our cabinets must take into account whether pastors can fluently speak the cultural vernacular of the inner-city families, upscale urban city dwellers, suburbanites, small town citizens, or rural residents of their communities. Pastors must also be fluent in the vernacular worship language of their church and their community, be it high church, contemporary, southern gospel, black gospel, or any number of variations of worship.

While moving frequently may remain common in the first years of ministry due to a high learning curve and the financial realities of young pastors providing for their growing families, steps must be taken to ensure pastors are placed as quickly as possible in ministry settings where they can effectively share the Gospel in the cultural vernacular.

As I learned in Southwest Virginia, remaining in one place for an extended period is crucial. Additionally, we can no longer give large strategic churches to pastors nearing retirement as a "thank you" for faithful years of service if those pastors do not possess the leadership skills to guide those congregations into a vibrant future.

Given the need for pastors to speak in the cultural vernacular of an increasingly diverse society, appointment making – never an easy task – is now more difficult than ever. As one former district superintendent said to me, "Appointment making is like working on a puzzle where all the pieces don't fit. You know they don't fit, and the best you can do is try to fit them together in such a way you can still see the basic outline of the puzzle when you are done."

To help put our pastors in position to maximize the effectiveness of their gifts, as well as the gifts of the local church, new methods of training will be required for bishops and district superintendents. Such areas as the art of human resource deployment, understanding local cultures and subcultures, assessing the gifts and strengths of their pastors to a much higher degree, and learning how to recruit new clergy with specialized skill sets and cultural affinities will be a necessity.

In this new appointment making paradigm, factors like salary and years of experience must still be taken into account. Failing to do so would be unwise and unfair. Rather than jettisoning these factors entirely, they must become part of a new equation with many other variables.

Raising up 21st century leaders

While there has been a necessary focus on raising up strong, effective pastoral leaders in recent years within United Methodism, the emphasis on developing effective bishops and district superintendents has not received as much energy.

The district superintendent is the basic link between our denomination and the local congregation. The 2012 Book of Discipline was wise to redefine the role of district superintendent to include being the chief "missional strategist" as a primary function.

In reality, the change from viewing the superintendent as the manager of the district clergy to the chief missional strategist, bearing primary responsibility for the vitality of the churches of the district, is a massive undertaking. It will require bishops to understand how to train superintendents in their new role, and create structures within our annual conferences to enable superintendents to carry out their duties. As long as our annual conferences' organizational structures remain the same, even the most astute superintendents will struggle with their new role.

Our changing culture necessitates our bishops and district superintendents move from being managers to becoming visionary leaders, leading our churches on a new course that leads to vibrant 21st century faith communities.

The good news is we already have bishops and district superintendents who have discerned how to be visionary leaders in many places throughout our connection. We have annual conference cabinet members who have explored the unspoken assumptions which often guide appointment making, creating wise and faithful methods to effectively match pastors and churches. The bad news is, as a denomination, we have yet to develop a standardized approach for sharing these lessons on a broad scale.

We must learn all we can, as quickly as we can, from our pioneering leaders. Our world is going through a revolution which is changing the relationship between our annual conferences and local congregations which, according to the Book of Discipline, are the primary places where disciples of Jesus Christ are formed.[2]

Our options are to adapt to these changes or be left behind.

---

2 The Book of Discipline of the United Methodist Church, 2016. Para. 201. p147.

So you say you want a revolution?

During Jesus' time, the world was in the midst of a technological revolution which would eventually decrease the cost and increase the speed of communication significantly. Without this revolution, the shape of early Christianity would have been dramatically different as it played a fundamental role in the spread of Christianity throughout the Roman world. The revolution of which we speak is the development of the codex book which replaced the scroll as the primary medium for long-form written communication.

The codex was first developed around the time of Jesus' birth. It decreased the cost of written communication because both sides of the page could be used. It also provided a more user-friendly experience by making it much easier to find and reference particular passages. Additionally, the codex's compact and durable format made it far easier to transport and distribute.

While it would take 600 years for the codex to fully overtake the scroll as the dominant format for long form writing in the Roman World, within the Christian community the codex replaced the scroll as the primary medium for writing by the 2nd century. The early adoption of this new technology allowed Christians to spread their writings quickly throughout the Mediterranean world. Some of these writings eventually came to comprise the New Testament.

The next major technological revolution to rival the codex occurred when a German goldsmith named

Johannes Gutenberg invented the printing press in 1440. This enabled mass production of books by combining movable type technology with existing screw-press manufacturing technology. The newly available and affordable texts made possible by the printing press helped spread knowledge throughout Europe at a previously unthinkable rate.

Not coincidentally, less than a century after the invention of the printing press, the Protestant Reformation swept across Europe. The Roman Catholic Church struggled with corruption and corrupt theology for centuries before Martin Luther kick-started the Reformation by posting his 95 Theses in 1517.

In previous centuries, there had been no shortage of saints and martyrs willing to give their lives to reform the church. What those early reformers lacked was a means to get their message to the common people. Martin Luther and his contemporaries could thank Mr. Gutenberg and his printing press for the ability to spread the Gospel at previously unthinkable speed.

Today, we are arguably in the third major communication revolution in communication technology since the time of Christ, the digital revolution. Within the last century our society transitioned from a society where mass communication took place primarily through printed publications to a society where most mass communication now takes place digitally, allowing thoughts to travel from one location to another instantly, with the push of a button.

Personal communication has quickly followed the lead of mass communication. Our newest generations will have little memory of how people communicated prior to email, text, social media, and video chats.

This new revolution has already revolutionized the relationship between annual conferences and their constituent churches. Churches which used to rely on annual conference or denominational mission directors to be involved in missions around the world now have personal partnerships and weekly communication with missionaries and partner churches across the globe. Church leadership expertise and ecclesiastical information, previously found only in denominational offices, now resides on the Internet and can be accessed any time day or night.

The institutional denominational hierarchies built to enable ministry in an earlier age now slow and sometimes even prevent ministry by creating an unruly system of checks and balances that must be satisfied before a new project can be approved. As churches increasingly work around and outside of official denominational hierarchy with these new tools at their disposal, great stress develops within denominational and annual conference program ministries which now seek to carry out their ministries with the support of fewer churches.

The wireless digital revolution will necessitate change among denominational boards and annual conferences. Considerations must be given to providing local churches with the necessary tools to be directly involved in mission and ministry, rather than directly leading and managing mission and ministry opportunities on behalf of the local churches.

While there will still be a more limited role for the

denomination in managing mission and ministry opportunities for smaller churches with limited resources, our system must allow for everyone, including small congregations, to develop direct leadership opportunities in these areas. Moreover, more understanding should be given to large churches who often find small-scale denominational ministries do not align with the emphases of their congregations.[3]

Beyond the changing nature of the relationship between churches and annual conferences, the wireless digital communications revolution has significantly changed the way pastors and churches reach their communities.

For decades churches had two primary ways to communicate with their members, the newsletter and the bulletin. They also had two primary ways to advertise to their community, the newspaper and billboards. While these methods still have some validity, churches must now have a multi-faceted communications strategy that utilizes numerous methods of reaching people.

The fact more people within the United States are being raised outside the faith, the decline of monthly church attendance among committed church members, and the diverse ways different generations wish to receive information should cause us to recognize the immensity of challenges facing not just United Methodism, but all churches.

---

3 For an excellent explanation of how new technology is redefining the nature of the relationship between annual conferences and local churches, see chapter 2 - "Why Working Harder Isn't Helping," of Bishop Robert Schnase's book, "Seven Levers: Missional Strategies for Conferences."

While attendance at UMC congregations, along with most other denominations, has decreased significantly over the past few decades, there is an encouraging trend of rapid growth among United Methodist churches in the global south. This leads to questions regarding the extent to which U.S. dollars fund ministry throughout the world, and the need to reform United Methodism to become a truly global church, rather a US-centric denomination. The stakes are clear.

On its own, any of the challenges listed in this chapter would require highly disciplined attention and a significant outlay of resources from our denomination. Combined, these challenges demand even more attention, energy, and resources as we work together at every level of the church to lead United Methodism into a season of renewal, revival, and growth.

Precious, but not priceless

As Protestants, we recognize Christian unity is precious, but not priceless. While Christian division hinders the spread of the Gospel, there are moments when the need to reform the church to accomplish its historic mission in a new age becomes so great that we must consider diverging ecclesiastical paths to do so.

Even if United Methodists can continue to agree on our basic theological tenets (as outlined in chapter 4), we must consider, at this unique moment in time, whether it is possible to find a way to remain united, while placing the majority of our energy and resources on the great challenges we face. Could unity at all costs lead us to become so distracted by our internal debates that we fail to reach out to the world into which Christ sent us to make disciples?

In John 13:35, Jesus says, "By this everyone will know that you are my disciples, if you love one another." (NIV)

You will notice he does not say the world will know his disciples by how they structure their ministry within a common denominational polity. There is nothing to fear in remaining united or splitting in a loving way. There is much to fear about remaining together or splitting with competition, jealously, and resentment in our hearts.

In the next chapter, we will take a personal and soul-searching look into our own hearts to discern whether we have allowed agendas other than love to compromise our witness. Furthermore, we will discuss what it means, in this day and age, to love one another as Christ has loved us.

Right now, I would ask you to join me in praying this prayer.

> Gracious Savior and Lord of Love,
> Watch over Your people called Methodist in these hours.
> Teach us to love alike when we do not think alike,
> to see Your presence in those we do not understand, and to trust in You to make a way for us to carry out Your great commission, even when the path ahead appears so uncertain.
> Whether we find ourselves united by church polity or only by the bond of Your Holy Spirit,
> help us to love one another in such a manner
> so the world might see You through us.
>
> Amen.

Chapter Six

What's Your Agenda?

"Never use the weapons of Satan against the people of God."

2016 General Conference
Bishop James Swanson, Mississippi Conference

"What's your agenda when you walk into the room? Someone tell me right now what your agenda is!" The intensity of my supervisor's voice caught me off guard.

I was in my last year of seminary and serving as a hospital chaplain. Each week we met to debrief together, but our meeting this particular week was different than most. Our supervisor was worked up about our mindset as we entered a room to visit a patient. None of us could answer the question he put to us. So we all just stared at our feet.

"Okay, how many people think the right answer is to say you do not have an agenda?" he asked. Most of us sheepishly raised our hands.

"Wrong," he replied. "Everyone has an agenda. If you're going to be a helpful presence to your patients, you need to be real clear about your agenda, and how you plan to carry it out."

I have never forgotten his words, and I'm pretty sure he was right. We all have agendas. With that in mind, let's consider what our personal agendas have been and what they need to be in the future as we address the division within United Methodism surrounding LGBTQ inclusion.

The weapons of Satan and the people of God

Bishop James Swanson gave one of the most memorable sermons at General Conference 2016 when he implored us to not allow the powers of evil to influence the way in which we relate to those who disagree with us about LGBTQ inclusion. Speaking to folks of every viewpoint, Swanson proclaimed, "It's all right for you to disagree with me, but it's not all right for you to hate me. It's all right for you to plot to win, but never use the weapons of Satan against the people of God."

Have there been times when you have compromised your values to help your viewpoint win the day? Have you cared more about winning a debate than loving your neighbor?

Have you spoken of those with differing viewpoints with disdain, rather than respectful disagreement? Have you looked at your brothers and sisters in Christ as the enemy? Have you intentionally tried to isolate, humiliate, or intimidate in the name of serving the church?

Here's a question for church professionals: Has your concern for your future career shaped your opinion about

LGBTQ inclusion? If it has, has your concern been a higher priority than right and wrong?

Have you wished to silence the most stringent voices from either side in hopes of maintaining unity? Have you looked at another Christian with hatred in your heart? Have you used the weapons of Satan against the people of God?

If you are like me, your answer to some of these questions is yes. Maybe not all of them, but more than you would like to admit. Thankfully, we find ourselves in good company.

During Jesus' life, Peter exhibited unquestionable passion for serving him. Even so, his passion was accompanied by rather questionable responses in a few pressure-filled situations. The 18th chapter of the Gospel of John tells us when the guards came to arrest Jesus, Peter was ready to fight to the death.

> 10 Then Simon Peter, who had a sword, drew it and struck the high priest's servant, cutting off his right ear. (The servant's name was Malchus.)
> 11 Jesus commanded Peter, "Put your sword away! Shall I not drink the cup the Father has given me?" (NIV)

Peter's passion for protecting Jesus caused him to abandon the values Jesus taught him and forsake the mission Jesus gave him. By taking up the sword, Peter had unknowingly become a greater hindrance to Jesus' ministry than the priests and soldiers who came to arrest Jesus.

If that was the only mistake Peter made that night, it might be easier to overlook. Just a few short hours later,

Peter would deny Christ three times to save his own skin. The man who was ready to fight to death for Christ, shied away in cowardice from the chance to stand up for Jesus in his greatest hour of need.

The Gospel of John spends only two chapters on Jesus' resurrection, chapters 20 and 21. Not coincidentally, almost the entirety of John 21 is dedicated to the repentance of Peter in the presence of the Risen Christ.

Consider the profound conversation between the Risen Jesus and Peter on the seashore recorded in John 21:

> 15 When they had finished eating, Jesus said to Simon Peter, "Simon son of John, do you love me more than these?"
> "Yes, Lord," he said, "you know that I love you."
> Jesus said, "Feed my lambs."
> 16 Again Jesus said, "Simon son of John, do you love me?"
> He answered, "Yes, Lord, you know that I love you."
> Jesus said, "Take care of my sheep."
> 17 The third time he said to him, "Simon son of John, do you love me?"
> Peter was hurt because Jesus asked him the third time, "Do you love me?" He said, "Lord, you know all things; you know that I love you."
> Jesus said, "Feed my sheep. 18 Very truly I tell you, when you were younger you dressed yourself and went where you wanted; but when you are old you will stretch out your hands, and someone else will dress you and lead you where you do not want to go." 19 Jesus said this to indicate the kind of death by which Peter would glorify God. Then he said to him, "Follow me!" (NIV)

In John's mind, he needed to do more than record the facts surrounding the Resurrected Jesus. It was equally important to be sure his readers understood the Risen Christ had brought repentance and reconciliation into the life of one of his closest disciples, possibly the one who had failed him the most.

You probably know how Peter's story ends. He becomes the unquestioned leader of the early church for several decades after Jesus' death. When threatened with crucifixion for his refusal to renounce his faith, Peter never asks for a reprievc. Instead he asks to be crucified upside down, because he did not feel worthy to die in the same manner as his Savior.

Of all the followers of Christ in the last 2000 years, only the Apostle Paul rivals Peter in terms of his influence on the world and the church.

If God is to use the people called United Methodists to influence and bless the world in the 21st century, it may depend on the willingness of all of us – traditionalists, centrists, and progressives – who have used the weapons of Satan against the people of God, to humbly confess and repent of our sins. We cannot preach repentance until we have ourselves repented. We cannot lead the world in revival until we ourselves have been revived.

Join me in an exercise: Find a piece of paper and jot down the ways you have been uncharitable to your neighbors of differing viewpoints. Write down the times you have cared more about winning the debate or vote than the well-being of your opponents. Identify the people or groups toward whom you harbor hatred and resentment.

Let's take it a step further and lift our sheets of paper to God in prayer. Confess your sins. Ask God to teach you anew to love your neighbors. Pray specifically for God to bless the very people and groups you have abhorred and resented.

Just as the Resurrected Christ asked Peter, "Do you

love me more than these?" spend time in prayer and listen to Christ ask you: "Do you love me more than winning the vote? Do you love spreading scriptural holiness more than getting your way? Do you love your neighbors more than your viewpoints?"

Remembering Jesus told a repentant Peter to feed his sheep, tell Jesus of your desire to treat all with the love, respect, and honor due a child of God.

After you have finished, come back and read the rest of this chapter.

An agenda for personal and social holiness

Now that we have asked some tough questions about our personal relationships with United Methodists of differing viewpoints, I want to challenge you to ask a difficult question about your motivation for serving the church. Think about your hopes for our denomination. Include hopes for your annual conference and local church.

Are you more concerned about helping people become more Christ-like or helping them to become more like you? Are you more focused on making disciples of Jesus Christ or on making others share your viewpoint?

Social and ethical teachings should always be an essential aspect of what it means to be a Christian. Any version of Christianity devoid of ethical teachings knows nothing of Christ and His teachings. However, ethical teachings will never be the core of Christianity. Christianity at its core is about a saving relationship with Jesus

112

Christ. This relationship provides a moral compass to help us discern right from wrong, good from evil. While Christians have gotten as far off the morality track as anyone else, a living relationship with Christ continually calls us back to truth and righteousness.

Even if we were to perfect our ethics for one brief moment in history, without Christ to guide us our morality would quickly falter in the midst of changing circumstances.

So I ask you again: Are you more interested in making followers of Christ or in making traditionalists, centrists, or progressives? History teaches us wherever Christ is proclaimed as Lord and Savior, even by those with incorrect ethical understandings, the kingdom of heaven draws near.

In the Antebellum South, slave owners made a frightening bargain with the Methodist circuit riders who came to preach to the slaves on their plantations. The circuit riders could gather the slaves for worship on the one condition: They would teach the slaves Jesus wanted them to be wholly obedient to their masters. For better or worse, many circuit riders took them up on the deal.

As the slaves began to accept the Gospel and receive the freedom and power it brings, they also began to question the validity of some of the politics included in the preaching. For this reason, they set up their own slave churches.

In these slave churches, human dignity was celebrated and the philosophical and organizational ground work was laid that, in years to come, would enable the black church to bless our country through its support of the underground railroad, abolition, and the civil rights movement.

The slaves may have been baptized into a corrupt version of Christianity, but God worked through their sincere faith to lead them into one of the most pure expressions of Christianity the world has ever seen.

As long as Christ remains the center of the Gospel, he will challenge and ultimately conquer the ethical misunderstandings and personal prejudices we mistakenly attach to it.

John Wesley and social holiness

John Wesley famously addressed the role of social holiness in the Gospel by saying, "The gospel of Christ knows of no religion but social; no holiness but social holiness."

In his use of the phrase "social holiness," Wesley did not mean holiness was nothing more than actively working for social reform or aggressively confronting the moral dilemmas of the day. His own life proves a holy life included personal piety, communal worship, study, and working for social reform.

Early in his life, Wesley worked voraciously on behalf of the poor and the oppressed. He visited prisons and worked intensely among the poor, all before having his conversion experience at Aldersgate, where he finally discovered a saving faith for himself.

Wesley knew as well as anyone good works on behalf

of social progress were not enough to sustain and save the human soul. He also knew good works and social justice were a fundamental ingredient of the Gospel of Jesus Christ.

After his conversion, Wesley worked even more diligently on behalf of the poor and oppressed. He started Methodist preaching houses in poor neighborhoods, preached in the fields to those without the proper attire to attend church, opened free medical clinics, sponsored feeding ministries, founded schools for impoverished children, promoted abolition, and conducted a direct assault on the prevailing logic of the day which taught poverty was a punishment for sin.

John Wesley did so much to change the social ethics of England in his time that some historians believe his influence may have prevented England from experiencing the kind of class-based revolution which occurred in France.

The social holiness of which Wesley spoke included worshiping and praying in church with other believers and working for social justice in the world. When Wesley said, "Christ knows no holiness, but social holiness," he meant in addition to our personal acts of piety, such as personal scripture reading, fasting, and prayer, we need edifying Christian fellowship through the church. He taught in addition to edifying fellowship, we also need to work together to bless the poor and oppressed in our world.

As Wesleyan Christians of various viewpoints, we cannot stop working on behalf of what we believe to be right when it comes to LGBTQ inclusion. To do so would be to forsake the very Wesleyan heritage through which we found a saving faith.

What we can do is make sure we are more concerned about sharing the truth of Christ than arguing among ourselves concerning issues on which we disagree.

Stopping the proxy wars

On the denominational level, the fight over LGBTQ inclusion has often been played out through proxy wars and power grabs. In these unfortunate instances, a side violates common principles to increase their chances of winning votes regarding LGBTQ inclusion.

With LGBTQ inclusion dominating everyone's agenda, the chances of reforming the church for effective ministry in the 21st century declines as necessary reforms are put off, due to concerns of tipping the balance of power. Whatever ultimately happens at the special 2019 General Conference focused on the issue of LGBTQ inclusion, a resolution must be reached to stop the proxy wars which are ending ministry before it begins.

One of the most important moments of the 2016 General Conference, as well as one of the briefest, came from the Connectional Table. The Connectional Table is a rather small representative body of the church charged with guiding the ministry of the denomination between General Conferences. It's not so different than the way a local church council will guide the work of a congregation between charge conferences. In their report to the 2016 General Conference, the Connectional Table shared their desire to spend the next four years wrestling with the question, "What does it mean to be a truly global church?" They hope to bring legislation in 2020 to help our structure become more global than our current system, which is set up for the old Methodist Church, an American church with a few international branches.

To me, the greatest question we have to answer as a denomination is, "Do we really want to be a global church?"

If we want to be a global church, then we must level the playing field between the United States and the Central (non-American) Conferences. This would involve discerning which freedoms local central conferences, and perhaps jurisdictions, should have, and making those freedoms uniform. This is in addition to continuing to work towards an equitable and sustainable way of paying the apportionments which fund the denomination.

In the coming years, the Connectional Table must help us establish what is truly essential and what practices are nonessential and require liberty to allow each annual conference and local churches to minister most effectively in their setting.

If we respond wisely, we can set ourselves up to be a truly global church in the 21st century. If we get this wrong, we will likely move from a US-centric church to an African-centric church. Then, in the next century, it's possible we might become Asian-centric. Regardless of which part of the world contains the most United Methodists, if we can correctly appreciate the essentials and nonessentials, we position ourselves for fruitful ministry throughout the world.

If not, it is almost certain we will set up a system where churches in minority cultures are not given the freedom they need to minister with maximum effectiveness. At worst, we will create a system which will eventually cause us to splinter into national churches. One of the challenges facing future General Conferences and the Connectional Table will be untangling many issues surrounding the global nature of the church that have become proxy wars over human sexuality. For instance, there was legislation brought before General Conference in 2016 to reform the formula for appointing delegates to General Conference. The idea is to bring the ratio of delegates more in line with the membership size of annual and central conferences.

However, in the short term this change would most likely mean more representation from demographics who often see human sexuality issues in a traditionalist manner. Many people who otherwise would support a more equitable formula for appointing delegates opposed it because of their concerns about human sexuality.

Additional legislation brought to the 2016 General Conference would have made the United States a central conference. While making the United States a central conference would probably be the simplest and most equitable way to begin to move from a US-centric church to a global church structure, there were many people who opposed any move in this direction out of fear it could create an avenue for American churches to become more liberal in their stances towards LGBTQ inclusion.

It's not hard to observe the conundrum in which we find ourselves. We are rapidly growing throughout the world and becoming a more diverse denomination. Our structures need to reflect this growth, but it is hard to make principled decisions regarding the global nature of the church when we are fighting proxy wars at every turn.

Faithfully facing the future or doomed to repeat the past

Whatever the results of our debate over LGBTQ inclusion, one fact is certain. This will not be the last time diverse opinions on the issues of the day will threaten the unity of our denomination.

Whether we split into separate denominations or remain united, it would behoove us to ask ourselves how we want our church to handle weighty social issues in the future, knowing the next time around we may find our opinions in the minority.

The current governance of the UMC is structured to have a strong legislature branch (General Conference), a strong judicial branch (Judicial Council), and a weak executive branch (Council of Bishops). Bishops have no voice or vote at General Conference, and the Council of Bishops cannot advise the General Conference without a request to do so from the conference itself.

In our current system, it is easy to experience the tyranny of the majority. With 51 percent of the vote, one side can entirely impose its will upon the 49 percent minority. Thus, many times debates get quite heated, since it is possible for a small majority to pass legislation that is entirely untenable to the large minority.

The United States dealt with these same issues when forming its government. For this reason, the United States chose to implement a strong executive branch, the President, and to divide its legislature into two houses, the House of Representatives and the Senate. The president helps to represent the minority because he or she is elected by the entire nation, not just a state or district.

The Senate also helps to give the minority a voice because each state gets an equal number of Senators, unlike the House of Representatives. Not surprisingly the House of Representatives often produces the most extreme legislation. For this reason, I seriously doubt many of us would be comfortable with a country that had only a House of Representatives without a Senate.

It is reported when the United States government was being formed in 1787 George Washington told Thomas Jefferson the purpose of creating the Senate was to "cool the hot tea of the House" in the same way a saucer provides a cool place to set a hot tea cup.

Washington's understanding was that the Senate should help make the more extreme legislation coming from the House of Representative milder by incorporating the needs of the minority to a greater degree.

In no way am I arguing that the UMC should suddenly create a denominational senate. However, this is largely the reason I was glad to the see the 2016 General Conference ask its bishops to lead in an unprecedented

fashion. We often complain about our bishops not leading in a strong manner. It is not that bishops are weak
leaders. Primarily, it is due to United Methodist bishops
having very little institutional authority to lead on the
denominational level.

United Methodist bishops are by far the most thor-
oughly vetted leaders in our denomination. They are
charged with ministering to the most diverse constituents and overseeing the worldwide ministries of the
denomination. When facing important matters that
threaten the very unity of our fellowship, it seems
unwise to fail to ask those who occupy the highest posts
to help guide us towards a path that addresses the concerns of all involved.

In whatever form Methodism exists in the years
ahead, it would do us all well to ask if giving our bishops more authority to lead would be fitting as we seek
to move faithfully into a future with plenty of its own
controversies and challenges.

You may disagree with me about the solutions I have
suggested in relation to the global nature of the church
and the need to protect and respect minority opinions.
I respect your differing opinions. It is entirely possible
you have much better solutions in mind.

Spend some time after reading this chapter to reflect
on your own views. How can our church become a truly
global church and how you would want the denomination to act if you found yourself to be in the minority
concerning one of the great social issues of the day?

Afterwards, we will reflect together about being

Christian witnesses when we find our opinions to be in the minority within our own congregation.

Chapter Seven

Becoming the
Loyal Opposition

*Those who wish to be first must put themselves last,
and those who wish to lead must first learn to follow.*

No church member ever made a more memorable first impression on me than Lisa. She was part of a large and tight-knit Sunday school class at the first church I served. Early in my tenure, I stopped by the class to introduce myself. After sharing a little about myself, I asked each person in the class to share their name and something they would like me to know about them.

When it was her turn, Lisa spoke out warmly. "I'm Lisa. I'm the only Democrat in this class and I enjoy setting all these Republicans straight."

The class erupted in laughter and from the knowing smiles of its members, I surmised Lisa was not exaggerating. There were other Sunday school classes in the church where Lisa would have found her political views to be in the majority, but this was her class.

This class edified her through the teaching, nourished her through life-long friendships, and loved her, even when she adamantly disagreed with the majority opinion.

Sadly, a few years later, Lisa became terminally ill. When I stopped by to see her in her last days, she told me of Sunday school class members who stopped by to visit, to bring a meal, or to help with an important errand. After Lisa's passing, I had countless conversations with members of her Sunday school class who wanted to tell me how much she meant to them.

Her humor and compassion left an indelible mark on those who knew her, as did her willingness to share her opinions and love with those with whom she disagreed. Many of those in Lisa's Sunday school class explained how much they respected her willingness to share her views, even when she was virtually alone in the minority. They appreciated how she challenged them to think more deeply about their own points of view, and how their relationship with her caused them to think more respectfully of those who disagreed with them.

The world could use a few more people like Lisa.

Preparing for an uncertain future

The actions of the General Conferences in 2019 and 2020 may force each United Methodist congregation to more openly define its stance towards LBGTQ inclusion. This dialogue will most likely cause some progressives and traditionalists to feel they need to move on to other churches more in line with their views. For many people who find themselves in the minority within their local church, the choice of leaving or staying will be excruciating.

You might find yourself in the minority within your congregation. If that's the case, consider if God is calling you to move on to another place as a prophetic act of leadership or if God is calling you to be a prophetic leader like Lisa, who remained true to her belief and truly loving to her faith community, even though her opinions were in the minority.

The loyal royal opposition

Perhaps no biblical figure demonstrates a more inspiring example of embracing his role as the loyal opposition than David. As a young man, David was anointed King of Israel by the prophet Samuel. Soon, thereafter, David went to the palace in Jerusalem not to lead a coup and overthrow King Saul who had turned away from God's guidance and lost God's favor, but instead to serve Saul.

David began his royal service as a harpist, comforting Saul with his music when he was tormented by evil spirits. Eventually David earned Saul's trust and was promoted to armor bearer for the king. After risking his own life to defeat Goliath on Saul's behalf, David became one of the most successful officers in Saul's army.

As David won victory after victory on the battlefield, Saul grew jealous of David's growing fame and popularity. Once, as David played the harp to calm Saul during a fit of rage, Saul threw his spear at David with the intent to kill him. David eluded the attack and remained loyal to Saul, continuing to lead Saul's army.

Sometime later, Saul's son, Jonathan, informed David his father's attack was not just a temporary lapse of sanity. Saul was actively plotting to have David assassinated.

At that moment, David knew he could no longer remain in Saul's service within the palace. So he set out to escape Saul's murderous rage by fleeing to the wilderness with only a small band of unlikely followers.

Saul pursued David aggressively with thousands of troops under his command. Yet David continually stayed a step ahead of Saul and slipped through his grasp time and again. At one point, when David was hiding in the wilderness of Engedi, Saul unknowingly entered the very cave where David was hiding. As Saul paused to relieve himself in the privacy of the cave, David and his men saw an opportunity to kill Saul. They probably knew David would likely be installed as king due to his popularity throughout Israel. Still, David called off his men and refused to harm a helpless Saul.

Instead, David uses the situation as an opportunity to demonstrate his loyalty to Saul once again. 1 Samuel 24: 8-22 records their timeless conversation.

> 8 Then David went out of the cave and called out to Saul, "My lord the king!" When Saul looked behind him, David bowed down and prostrated himself with his face to the ground. 9 He said to Saul, "Why do you listen when men say, 'David is bent on harming you'? 10 This day you have seen with your own eyes how the Lord delivered you into my hands in the cave. Some urged me to kill you, but I spared you; I said, 'I will not lay my hand on my lord, because he is the Lord's anointed.' 11 See, my father, look at this piece

of your robe in my hand! I cut off the corner of your robe but did not kill you. See that there is nothing in my hand to indicate that I am guilty of wrongdoing or rebellion. I have not wronged you, but you are hunting me down to take my life. 12 May the Lord judge between you and me. And may the Lord avenge the wrongs you have done to me, but my hand will not touch you. 13 As the old saying goes, 'From evildoers come evil deeds,' so my hand will not touch you.

14 "Against whom has the king of Israel come out? Who are you pursuing? A dead dog? A flea? 15 May the Lord be our judge and decide between us. May he consider my cause and uphold it; may he vindicate me by delivering me from your hand."

16 When David finished saying this, Saul asked, "Is that your voice, David my son?" And he wept aloud. 17 "You are more righteous than I," he said. "You have treated me well, but I have treated you badly. 18 You have just now told me about the good you did to me; the Lord delivered me into your hands, but you did not kill me. 19 When a man finds his enemy, does he let him get away unharmed? May the Lord reward you well for the way you treated me today. 20 I know that you will surely be king and that the kingdom of Israel will be established in your hands. 21 Now swear to me by the Lord that you will not kill off my descendants or wipe out my name from my father's family."

22 So David gave his oath to Saul. Then Saul returned home, but David and his men went up to the stronghold.

David had every right to take the throne from Saul by force. God had anointed David King. Saul had betrayed him and attempted to kill him. The people loved David and were ready for a new leader.

Instead, David used this event as an opportunity to demonstrate his faithfulness and trustworthiness to such an extraordinary degree that even Saul agreed David should be his successor. Through David, we see an example of Jesus' teaching: Those who wish to be first must put themselves last, and those who wish to lead must first learn to follow.

David remained in the palace serving Saul long after common sense would have led him to flee. Only when he had no other options did he leave the palace to preserve his life.

If you find yourself at odds with your local church over LGBTQ inclusion, you would do well to ask yourself, "Do I have other options besides leaving that would allow me to live out a faithful Christian witness?

John Wesley's Anglican opposition

From the time of John Wesley's dramatic Aldersgate experience, he fell out of favor with the Anglican hierarchy. Preaching a message that priests needed to get saved first if they wanted their church to experience revival got him kicked out of most pulpits and his exposure of the systemic injustices of British society won him few friends in the beginning.

As Wesley traveled from town to town preaching in the market squares, however, his gospel of practical divinity caught on like wildfire among the common folk. By making the Gospel accessible through his preaching, first by starting small groups to deepen faith then by training lay preachers and establishing Methodist Preaching Houses to engage the early Methodists in ministry to the poor and oppressed, Wesley led a revival on the outskirts of Anglicanism.

Late in his life, when the Anglican Church refused to prioritize ministry in the newly formed United States, Wesley directed Thomas Coke and Francis Asbury to establish the Methodist church in the United States as a separate entity from the Anglican church. Though he was directly responsible for the creation of this new denomination, Wesley himself remained an Anglican until his death. Most likely he felt, even though there was a missional need for a separate Methodist denomination in the newly formed United States, the same was not the case in England where Anglican investment in ministry was predictably strong.

If a day comes when you find yourself in the minority within your congregation, you may want to reflect on John Wesley's Anglicanism before leaving. Has the situation in your community reached such a point that the only way for you to be involved in fruitful ministry is to leave your church for a new church, or is it possible for you to remain a faithful member of your local church in good conscience even while supporting other expressions more in line with your understanding of the moral implications of the Gospel?

You and your local church

The local church is the primary place where disciples are made, not because the United Methodist Book of Discipline says so, but because we have learned this from centuries of experience. Many of us know the local church is where our faith and life come together. It is where we learn to worship, where we find edifying Christian fellowship, and where we are challenged to use our gifts to bless our world. The local church forms our deepest friendships and our deepest beliefs.

Though it sometimes appears weak, poor, and fragile, the local congregation is the glue holding the Christian movement together. If every denominational structure ceased to exist before next Sunday, Christians would still gather to worship.

Someone would preach. Someone would lead singing. Someone would organize missions. Someone would teach each small group and someone would bring a friend who did not know Christ to experience Christian love.

The local church is where we are married and buried. It is where we profess our faith and where mentors often help us discern our profession. We are baptized in the local church and we live out our baptism by venturing out to serve our world. When our lives fall apart, the local church holds us together. When our careers take off, the local church keeps our feet on the ground.

The local church contains vast networks of Christians seeking to love and support one another. When someone gets sick, visits are arranged. When someone has a baby, meals show up on the doorstep. When someone loses a job, calls are made to help find a new one. When someone's life spins out of control, loving confrontations from trusted friends help restore sanity. When someone can't afford to go to college, scholarships are sought out on their behalf. When a family can no longer pay their medical bills for a catastrophic illness, fund raisers are organized.

The local church is the most significant disciple-making arena because it is the primary arena through which we learn to love one another. Denominations rise and fall.

Worship styles change. The local church will remain until the end of time.

Your local church is one of God's greatest gifts to you and you are one of the God's greatest gifts to your local church. Before you leave your church, ask yourself if leaving over one issue is worth sacrificing all the support systems and friendships you have developed over years of serving God together.

One helpful paradigm for discerning whether to leave or stay at your local church might be to ask yourself if your disagreement with your local church has made the church a toxic place or just an uncomfortable place due to this one issue. If the church is toxic and you cannot in good conscience worship there without feeling like you are promoting a false version of the Gospel, then perhaps you need to find a new place where you can worship in good conscience. I have known numerous people who left their local churches for dozens of reasons. For them, finding a new church they could fully support proved to be good for them and good for their previous church.

Others discover, while they think their church is handling a particular issue in an unhealthy manner, they might be called to stay and support their church in other ways. They often become some of the most respected leaders in the local church because church members know they are putting the needs of the church above their own desires. Their lives bear witness to the truth that our unity in Christ transcends our disagreements.

In future years if you discover your congregation has become toxic for you, my prayers are with you as you venture out to find a new church home. Before you leave, however, I would suggest you should fervently pray about whether you could faithfully remain within your current church.

The world really could use a few more people like Lisa in it. Maybe you could be such a person in your local church.

Chapter Eight

Church Unity

All I ever needed to know about church unity,
I learned from a nondenominational pastor

The greatest obstacles we have to overcome
are within our own hearts.

As the divisions threatening the unity of United Methodism became clear during the 2016 General Conference,
my delegation from the Holston Annual Conference gathered together to pray for the unity of the church. During
our time of prayer, Rev. Carol Wilson reminded us, "From
the beginning of Christianity, the human polities adopted
to govern the life of the church have never been able to
fully encompass the diversity of Christians created by
the indwelling of the Holy Spirit for the fulfilment of the
church triumphant."

Her profound words reminded us that, whether the
United Methodist Church remains united through a
shared denominational polity or not, we would remain
united through the much stronger bond of the Holy
Spirit. Though the United Methodist Church may face a

division, there is no division in the Kingdom of God.

So long as we are united by the One Spirit as citizens of the One Kingdom, then shared ministry with other Christians whose theology and ethics are slightly different from our own is possible. In fact, it's not only possible, it is essential in carrying out the Kingdom's cause on earth.

Only one thing can prevent the people currently called United Methodists from continuing to work together for the cause of Christ in our world, regardless of our future denominational polity decisions: Our own pride and sinfulness.

I know this to be true because of what I learned from a dear friend and nondenominational pastor.

Lessons from a life well lived

When I came to pastor Lebanon Memorial United Methodist Church in Lebanon, Virginia in 2010, I soon met Jeff Williams, pastor of Lebanon Community Fellowship (LCF), a vibrant, growing nondenominational church just down the road. Jeff took me out to lunch, shared his story of struggles and victories in life and ministry, and assured me he was my "No. 1 fan," and praying for the ministry of my church. He did all this before he hardly even knew me. I quickly learned he wasn't being insincere. This was just Jeff being Jeff.

One of the toughest phone calls of my professional life was to Jeff. Over the years, he and I had come to share a mutual admiration for one another and discovered we each shared a passion for recovery ministry. We felt our community desperately needed a recovery ministry, but didn't want to launch competing ministries in a small town. After several conversations, it became apparent LCF was not ready to launch a ministry in the near future and my church made the decision to begin.

As the time of the launch neared, we felt we had everything we needed for a successful ministry, except a good band. So one day, after taking a few deep breaths, I picked up the phone and called Jeff. Not surprisingly, his church happened to have a first-rate worship band.

I asked Jeff if I could borrow one musician who could play guitar and sing. At this point, any musician would help.

For those who don't know, asking a pastor to share a musician is kind of like asking a baseball coach to share his best pitcher. It's a big request.

I'll never forget Jeff's response, "Wil, not only will I give you a musician, I will give you my whole band, myself, and my whole church. We will serve your church in order to serve our community.

His next request caused me to grin.

"Just don't tell my band about this. They don't know they are going to do it yet."

I don't know what Jeff told his band but it must have been good. I have rarely been a part of something as fulfilling and inspiring as serving alongside Jeff and the LCF band in the Recovery at Lebanon ministry that came to be as a result of our partnership.

Jeff had a schedule as busy as anyone in town, yet he

showed up every Thursday to do anything he could to help others find freedom from addiction. His payoff was seeing the joy that comes with faith.

Often Jeff and I would sit around and talk about the challenges facing Christianity in our culture and the challenges facing each of our churches. In these conversations, I learned Jeff had wisely chosen to recklessly pursue God's calling in his life.

Jeff greatly respected the denominational tradition in which he began his ministry, but when denominational politics threatened to stifle the mission to which he felt called, he bravely stepped out on faith to plant a new nondenominational church. He shepherded LCF through lean years of struggle when the future was uncertain, while resisting the temptation of greener pastures. He could have easily found a higher salary elsewhere, but he knew this was his pasture.

Jeff had an encouraging spirit. I have rarely encountered anyone like him. He was always smiling. He was always encouraging. He believed God was always ready to work miracles. I saw this spirit in his interactions with folks who were locked in life and death struggles as a result of their addictions.

I saw it in his interactions with me. I can't imagine what Jeff, a busy pastor at a large growing church, could get out of a relationship with a much younger pastor at a smaller church. We weren't even in the same denomination.

Thankfully, Jeff didn't look at our relationship that way. I'm pretty sure he just saw us as two guys, desperately trying to follow God, love our families, and lead our churches.

It wasn't unusual in our conversations for Jeff to ask my opinion about tough decisions facing his church. I learned Jeff's encouraging spirit was accompanied by a keen intellect. He read widely. His thoughts concerning faith were on the deepest levels. He was driven to grow, and to help others grow, to be conformed into the likeness of Christ.

In all honesty, Jeff and I read our Bibles somewhat differently. Our theological beliefs had some subtle, but substantial differences, and our churches came from different branches of Christianity. Somehow, those things didn't seem to matter too much to Jeff. Somewhere along the way, he became infatuated with the calling of Christ to love one another as He loved us.

As our churches began working even closer together for the good of our community, it was not unusual for strangers to share how inspired they were by witnessing two churches working so well together. Some people even shared that seeing our churches selflessly share ministry caused them to rekindle their faith and go back to church again after many years of being away.

Today in Lebanon, Virginia, there are people living who would have died of a drug overdose, because two churches and two pastors chose to work together. There are people who have decent jobs and custody of their children because two churches chose to share ministry.

There are people who never thought they could live without mind-altering pills who are now pillars of their community, all because they found a saving faith in Jesus Christ when two churches decided to care more about saving souls than maintaining or growing membership rolls.

The greatest obstacles we had to overcome were within our own hearts. My pride almost sabotaged our success before we even began. I found it extremely difficult to humble myself enough to call Jeff and ask for his help. I wanted to show the community our church could do it on our own.

On the other hand, if Jeff had an ounce of self-interest in his heart, our recovery ministry would never have happened. Acting on faith, his church poured volunteers and resources into a ministry that gave them no obvious benefits in return.

Thankfully, over the course of his life, Jeff's self-interests had been transformed by God's love into "Kingdom interests." Whenever I would express gratitude for all the support of LCF, Jeff would remind me my church had given his church the greatest gift, an opportunity to serve selflessly.

I now serve a different congregation in a larger city. Still, I wish I could have lunch with Jeff and ask him what he thinks the United Methodist Church should do about its conflict over LGBTQ inclusion.

Sadly, I can't. Just a couple months after I moved to my current appointment, Jeff was diagnosed with terminal cancer. In the spring of 2016, just a few months after his diagnosis, Jeff passed away. I often reflect on what God taught me about Christian unity through my good friend, Jeff.

If I take anything away from my experiences working with Jeff and his church, it is that denominational structures cannot stop local churches from working together for the good of the Kingdom of God. But unchecked pride, greed, jealousy, and self-interest, growing in the hearts of church leaders, will stop ministry in its tracks every time.

Missing the mark

Like many of us, Jesus' disciples learned this lesson the hard way. Luke 9:49-50 tells us of their initial response to discovering a stranger casting out demons in the name of Jesus.

> 49 "Master," said John, "we saw someone driving out demons in your name and we tried to stop him, because he is not one of us."
>
> 50 "Do not stop him," Jesus said, "for whoever is not against you is for you." (NIV)

Look closely at this passage and consider the absurdity of the response of the disciples. They had just discovered a stranger casting out demons in Jesus' name.

Do they stop to celebrate? No. Do they get to know the person and learn his story? No.

Do they talk to the people who have been healed about their response to God's miraculous work? No.

It never occurs to the disciples to celebrate God's miracles. Instead, they become concerned because the person through whom God is working.

In other words, he was not one of them. He was a different kind of Christian, so they told him to stop working miracles. Then, to make matters worse, John had the

139

audacity to tell Jesus what they have done.

Can you believe it? The disciples would rather people remain sick and demon-possessed than be healed through someone they don't know. They are so full of pride and arrogance that they became more concerned about following the proper established channels than saving lives and souls.

Jesus had every right to rip into his disciples for their shallow response. This seems like another excellent moment for him to pull out that "Get behind me, Satan" line he used so effectively on Peter.

Instead, he simply corrects the disciples saying, "Do not stop him; for whoever is not against you is for you." (Luke 9:50 NIV)

Jesus cares about saving people. His disciples care about preserving their image. Jesus cares about connecting human souls with God. His disciples care about making sure no one comes to know God outside of their influence. Thankfully, Jesus settles the issue quickly and definitively.

Wouldn't it be nice if we could rejoice over miraculous ministry being perform by Christians with slightly different beliefs?

Have you ever resented other churches? Have you ever spoken dismissively of practices and miracles that occur in churches that practice differently than your church?

Have you ever wished ill on another church because you strongly disagreed with their reaction to the controversial issues of the day?

Yes, the problem with Jesus' first disciples is a problem with Jesus' disciples today. How much we, in the United Methodist Church, need to hear Jesus' sobering words, "Do not stop [them]; for whoever is not against you is for you."

Fear, faith and the future

John Wesley famously said:

> "I am not afraid that the people called Methodists should ever cease to exist either in Europe or America. But I am afraid lest they should only exist as a dead sect, having the form of religion without the power. And this undoubtedly will be the case unless they hold fast both the doctrine, spirit, and discipline with which they first set out."

I do not fear the division of the United Methodist Church. I fear, whether we remain together or divide, we will resent and undermine those Methodists who see things differently from us. I fear we will fail to work together in ministry because we secretly wish those Methodists of other viewpoints would cease and desist from identifying themselves as Methodists at all.

I also fear we will allow our denominational squabbles to needlessly distract our local churches from their mission to make disciples in their local communities.

The masses of people in our world who do not know Jesus Christ are not concerned with the internal squabbles of United Methodism. They are keenly concerned with finding a life full of hope, grace, and meaning.

The millions of people in our world who are battling

the demons of disease, addiction, isolation, and extreme poverty are not waiting for a perfectly organized denomination to reach them. They are waiting for local Christians in local churches to love them.

May we, the people called United Methodists, recommit ourselves now and in the future to share Christ with our local communities, working together whenever possible to offer Christ's miraculous saving presence to our broken and hurting world.

Like Jeff did for my congregation in Southwest Virginia, may we pray God's blessings upon those of other viewpoints and their churches, even if our consciences force our paths to diverge.

There is one truth I learned from Jeff above all. It is not about us. It is about God. By resisting the temptation to seek our own good at the expense of our brothers and sisters with different practices, we can grow to heights previously unknown.

We serve a limitless Lord. Let us not limit God by limiting ourselves.

Conclusion

My Prayer

For You, Me, and the UMC

In his sermon, "The One Thing Needful," John Wesley describes the only true need of humanity as being restored to the image of God.

The Gospel of John puts the matter in slightly different language by stating:

> Now this is eternal life: that they know you, the only true God, and Jesus Christ, whom you have sent. (John 17:3, NIV)

In contemporary American English, we might describe the one needful thing as a living, saving personal relationship with Jesus Christ.

These times of conflict and possible division are difficult and traumatic for all committed United Methodists. They can be especially hard for those who recently found faith in Christ through the United Methodist Church and wonder why their Christian brothers and sisters cannot

143

find strength through the Holy Spirit to remain united in effective ministry.

My hope for all who read this book is you find your personal faith strengthened, your respect for those who read the Gospel differently increased, and your understanding of United Methodist history and governance enhanced. My goal in writing has been to care for the souls of United Methodists of all viewpoints who find their denomination in the midst a tumultuous crisis unlike any other in our lifetime.

I truly believe the issues, which we now see through a mirror dimly, will become clear one day, or at least clear to our great grandchildren. In the meantime, my prayer is that we courageously hold fast to the one needful thing, even as our church structure bends and shakes in this historic storm.

When the winds and waves became so great that Jesus' disciples were sure they would perish, they looked around and found Christ calmly sleeping in the boat.

Christ is with us. We need not be afraid. Nor should we be ashamed.

In Romans 1:16, Paul dramatically states,

> For I am not ashamed of the gospel, because it is the power of God that brings salvation to everyone who believes: first to the Jew, then to the Gentile. (NIV)

We need not be ashamed today of the United Methodist proclamation of the Gospel. Those United Methodists who proclaim the Gospel from a traditionalist perspective do so out of a sincere desire to share the truth of God. This alone can lead to eternal fulfillment.

Those who share the Gospel from a progressive perspective do so from a devout commitment to share the truth that all God's children are beautifully created in God's image.

Those who share the Gospel from a centrist perspective do so out of a deeply seated yearning to see the church unified in life-giving mission and ministry.

Our differences of opinion are real and have life altering consequences for the people of our communities. Even so, our differences pale in comparison to the power of the One Spirit which unites us in the One Church of the One Lord.

May we face the future with a faith that makes us unafraid to treat those of differing opinions with charitable grace and unashamed of the Gospel which calls us to share Christ with a world in great need of His healing power.

Acknowledgments

I am thankful for the staff and members of Concord
United Methodist Church for their whole-hearted ministry
to our community and their enthusiastic support of this
writing project. My gratitude will always be with the
people of Middlebrook Pike UMC and Lebanon Memorial
UMC who invited me into their lives and their churches.

The clergy of the Holston Conference have repeatedly
honored and humbled me by asking me to serve in leadership roles in hopes that I might add something of value
to our denominational conversations. Representing my
colleagues in debates that affect the future ministry of
their churches is one of the highest professional honors
and greatest responsibilities I can imagine.

My thoughts on faith and United Methodism were
greatly enriched by the many United Methodist leaders
who spoke at length with me about their ideas, hopes,

and fears for our denomination as I prepared to write this book.

I am grateful to the small band of strong leaders in my clergy covenant small group who for years have helped keep my heart in love with Christ, my feet on the ground, and my head on straight by caring more about the condition of my soul than the state of my ministry.

Kevin Slimp and Market Square Publishing immediately saw the value in the message of *Unafraid and Unashamed* and worked tirelessly to remove every obstacle that would prevent this book from reaching its audience in a timely manner. In the process of developing this work, Jean Henderson's editing expertise proved invaluable.

Numerous colleagues and United Methodist leaders selflessly read and re-read manuscripts of this work to help me communicate with clarity and charity. Among them, Rev. Paul Seay and Rev. Don Hanshew provided writing advice and encouragement without which I would not have had the resolve or opportunity to pursue this project.

Finally, thanks to my family. Growing up, my parents and grandparents, as well as my sister and extended family, demonstrated to me the unrivaled power of combining personal and social holiness through their daily lives.

My wife, Rebecca, blesses me constantly with her love

and wisdom. Her care for the people of the United Methodist Church and belief in the ideas within this book are evidenced in the text of each page. My children inspire so much of what I do as their lives cause me to dream of a day when they will be able to raise their children in a United Methodist Church unafraid and unashamed of the Gospel of our Lord.

Wil Cantrell
Author, *Unafraid and Unashamed*